THE LETTER AND THE SPIRIT

THE LETTER AND THE SPIRIT

EIGHT LECTURES

DELIVERED BEFORE

THE UNIVERSITY OF OXFORD

IN THE YEAR MDCCCLXXXVIII.

ON THE FOUNDATION OF

THE LATE REV. JOHN BAMPTON, M.A.

CANON OF SALISBURY

BY

ROBERT EDWARD BARTLETT, M.A.

LATE FELLOW AND TUTOR OF TRINITY COLLEGE

London

RIVINGTONS, WATERLOO PLACE

New York

E. & J. B. YOUNG & COMPANY

COOPER UNION, FOURTH AVENUE

MDCCCLXXXVIII

EXTRACT

FROM THE LAST WILL AND TESTAMENT

OF THE LATE

REV. JOHN BAMPTON,

CANON OF SALISBURY.

" . . . I give and bequeath my Lands and Estates to the Chancellor, Masters, and Scholars of the University of Oxford for ever, to have and to hold all and singular the said Lands or Estates upon trust, and to the intents and purposes hereinafter mentioned; that is to say, I will and appoint that the Vice-Chancellor of the University of Oxford for the time being shall take and receive all the rents, issues, and profits thereof, and (after all taxes, reparations, and necessary deductions made) that he pay all the remainder to the endowment of eight Divinity Lecture Sermons, to be established for ever in the said University, and to be performed in the manner following:

"I direct and appoint, that, upon the first Tuesday in Easter Term, a Lecturer be yearly chosen by the Heads of Colleges only, and by no others, in the room adjoining to the Printing-House, between the hours of ten in the morning and two in the afternoon, to preach eight Divinity Lecture Sermons, the year following, at St. Mary's in Oxford, between the commencement of the last month in Lent Term, and the end of the third week in Act Term.

"Also I direct and appoint, that the eight Divinity Lecture Sermons shall be preached upon either of the following Subjects—to confirm and establish the Christian Faith, and to confute all heretics

a 3

and schismatics—upon the divine authority of the holy Scriptures—upon the authority of the writings of the primitive Fathers, as to the faith and practice of the primitive Church—upon the Divinity of our Lord and Saviour Jesus Christ—upon the Divinity of the Holy Ghost —upon the Articles of the Christian Faith, as comprehended in the Apostles' and Nicene Creeds.

" Also I direct, that thirty copies of the eight Divinity Lecture Sermons shall be always printed, within two months after they are preached ; and one copy shall be given to the Chancellor of the University, and one copy to the Head of every College, and one copy to the Mayor of the city of Oxford, and one copy to be put into the Bodleian Library ; and the expense of printing them shall be paid out of the revenue of the Land or Estates given for establishing the Divinity Lecture Sermons ; and the Preacher shall not be paid, nor be entitled to the revenue, before they are printed.

" Also I direct and appoint, that no person shall be qualified to preach the Divinity Lecture Sermons, unless he hath taken the degree of Master of Arts at least, in one of the two Universities of Oxford or Cambridge ; and that the same person shall never preach the Divinity Lecture Sermons twice."

CONTENTS

LECTURE I.

INTRODUCTION.

LECTURE II.

THE LETTER AND THE SPIRIT IN SCRIPTURE EXEGESIS.

LECTURE III.

THE LETTER AND THE SPIRIT IN SCRIPTURE EXEGESIS—(*continued*).

CONTENTS

LECTURE IV.

THE LETTER AND THE SPIRIT IN THE CHURCH.

LECTURE V.

THE LETTER AND THE SPIRIT IN THE SACRAMENTS.

LECTURE VI.

THE LETTER AND THE SPIRIT IN CREEDS AND CONFESSIONS OF FAITH.

LECTURE VII.

THE LETTER AND THE SPIRIT IN CHRISTIAN WORSHIP AND LIFE.

LECTURE VIII.

THE CHURCH OF THE FUTURE.

LECTURE I.

INTRODUCTION.

"Who also made us sufficient as ministers of a New Covenant; not of the letter, but of the spirit: for the letter killeth, but the spirit giveth life."—2 COR. iii. 6 (R.V.).

THE heavenly vision which appeared to Saul of Tarsus on the way as he journeyed to Damascus was not a mere turning-point in his life; rather it was the abrupt ending of one life, and the beginning of another. He was indeed the same man, with the same absolute devotion to the cause that he believed to be true, the same strange compound of weakness and strength, the same man as an Apostle that he had been as a persecutor of Christ: but he had been converted, turned about; he saw all things from an opposite point of view; what things had been gain to him, those he counted loss; old things were passed away, and all things were become new.

This fault in the strata of his life explains one of the most noticeable characteristics of his phraseology. With such a breach of continuity in his thoughts and experiences, it was natural that all things should seem to him double one against another; and that his ideas

B

should range themselves in antithetical form, and
embody themselves in opposite poles, coinciding with
his old and his new life. Thus, law and grace, faith
and works, faith and sight, sin and grace, death and
life, the old man and the new man, the flesh and the
spirit, the letter and the spirit—these became to St. Paul
centres around which fresh associations are continually
grouping themselves, and receive continually fresh
accessions of meaning as his thought moves onward.
This no doubt is what Luther means when he says that
St. Paul's words are like living creatures having hands
and feet; that they draw around themselves fresh
connotations, and grow and adapt themselves to fresh
uses. So that we are never sure that we have grasped
the whole of his thought; his words are like rays of
light, which contain many blended colours, and which
we must analyze by some intellectual prism, before they
will yield their full meaning to us. And even then, we
have further to reckon with the later associations which
modern use has drawn around them. Righteousness,
faith, law, grace, justification—terms like these elude our
comprehension all the more easily, because we begin by
attaching to them our modern associations, and fancying
that to St. Paul they meant no more and no less than
they mean to the writer or the reader of an English
book of devotion. How many theological misunder-
standings and confusions have arisen from these idols
of the market,[1] or—may we not say?—of the Church!

---

[1] "Idols of the market." Cf. Bacon, "Nov. Org.," I. lix: "The
Idols of the Market are the most troublesome of all, those namely

How much of our modern religious terminology is but the working up into a new building of stones shaped by Apostolic hands for quite other purposes! How often does the chemistry of theologians precipitate into hard and rigid forms the delicate spirituality of St. Paul's thoughts! How difficult we find it to divest ourselves of prepossessions, and to find in St. Paul's language the meaning, neither more nor less, which he intended to convey to those to whom he wrote!

I propose to take for the subject of these lectures one of those antitheses which, as we have seen, are so characteristic of St. Paul, the Letter and the Spirit. I shall endeavour, by a discussion of the passages in his writings in which they occur, to bring out the full meaning of the terms as he originally conceived of them. This will lead us on to the further question of their adoption into the theological vocabulary of early Christian writers, and so to that later and popular use by which they have come to mean the outward and the inward, the form and the substance, the transitory and the permanent, the accidental and the essential, in religion; and then to endeavour to discriminate these two elements in religious thought and life. Before entering on this wider field, it will be necessary to discuss with some fulness the use of the words in St. Paul's writings.

which have entwined themselves round the understanding from the associations of words and names. For men imagine that their reason governs words, whilst, in fact, words re-act upon the understanding."

The earliest passage in which the words occur is that in the third chapter of the Second Epistle to the Corinthians. He had been boasting that to him at least letters of commendation were unnecessary ; he needed no written documents to make good his claim to their obedience. They themselves were his only letter of commendation—a letter written, not with ink, but with the Spirit of the Living God ; not in tables of stone, but in tables that are hearts of flesh. But it is in no spirit of self-exaltation or self-sufficiency that he writes to them. His sufficiency is from God, Who had made him sufficient as a minister of a new Covenant—a minister not of letter, but of spirit ; for the letter killeth, but the spirit maketh alive. Here, then, he contrasts the old covenant with the new in this respect—that the one is letter, γράμμα ; the other is spirit, πνεῦμα. And we shall not fully enter into the significance of this contrast until we remember that to St. Paul the new Covenant of which he was a minister was absolutely without written documents. The conception of Christianity as intended to be, like the later Judaism, the religion of a book seems altogether foreign to his mind. The free spirit is to him the direct antithesis of the fixed and unprogressive letter. The διάκονοι γράμματος—ministers of letter—whom he contrasts with διάκονοι πνεύματος, would be persons whose function it was to administer a system of written rules, of punctilious observances, of formulas and rubrics, and whose great object it would be to produce conformity to a single outward type. Such was the system under which St. Paul had himself

been trained; as touching the law, a Pharisee; as
touching the righteousness which is in the law, found
blameless.[1] He had been instructed according to the
strict manner of the law of the Fathers.[2] But Christ
had revealed Himself to him, and the things that were
gain to him, those he now counted loss for Christ.[3] Old
things had passed away; all things had become new.[4]
The Law, which was ordained to life, he had found to be
unto death. Sin, taking occasion by the commandment, had slain him.[5] And so St. Paul, in his vivid
way, always identifies the Law with sin and death, the
Gospel with righteousness and life. " I had not known
sin," he says, " but by the Law." [6] Evil, no doubt, was
in him and around him; but not till the Law came, not
till the commandment awakened the consciousness of
sin, did sin take the definite form of opposition to the
Law. And that was all that the Law could do. The
Law was weak through the flesh. Its instruments, its
methods, were not spiritual, but carnal; it needed a new
law—the law of the Spirit of life in Christ Jesus,[7] to
make him free from the old Law—the law of sin and
death. And therefore the letter, the Law written and
engraven on stones, killeth. It can only reveal to a
man his sin, his spiritual bankruptcy, without giving
him any new principle of life, without lifting him up
and setting him on his feet again. But St. Paul had
been made a minister of the Spirit; of that new principle

---

[1] Phil. iii. 5, 6.   [2] Acts xxii. 3.   [3] Phil. iii. 7.
[4] 2 Cor. v. 17.   [5] Rom. vii. 10, 11.   [6] Rom. vii. 7.
[7] Rom. viii. 2.

of life which Christ had come to bring into the world ;
of that quickening Spirit, the Spirit of the Living God,
Which is not a law but a Life, impalpable, all-pervading,
Whose very Name is taken from the wind which bloweth
where it listeth,[1] the free breath of God, the Spirit of
Him that raised up Jesus from the dead.[2]   And therefore, while as a Hebrew he speaks of the Law with
national pride,—while he claims for the Jews much
advantage, because to them had been committed the
oracles of God,[3]—while he acknowledges the Law, so far
as it was ancillary to the yet older covenant which was
confirmed before by God,[4] to be holy and just and good,
—yet when it becomes a rival to the Covenant of Grace,
when it is represented as the final expression of God's Will,
he regards it with something like hostility, as working
wrath,[5] as bringing death,[6] as the strength of sin.[7]   And
when we remember what his experience had been, how
Christ had delivered him from the curse of the Law,[8] can
we wonder if he regarded the letter, the rigid, fixed,
hard, written Law, which he associated with the barren
discipline of his early life, as the very opposite principle
to the Spirit of life in Christ Jesus which had made him
free ?   Can we wonder if the letter and the spirit, when
he had once contrasted them, became to him symbols of
two principles of which the one was life and the other
death ?

[1] John iii. 8.   [2] Rom. viii. 11.   [3] Rom. iii. 2.

[4] Gal. iii. 17.   St. Augustine points out (" Contra Duas Ep.
Pelag.") that the New Testament is the older of the two.

[5] Rom. iv. 15.   [6] Rom. vii. 10.   [7] 1 Cor. xv. 56.

[8] Gal. iii. 13.

It is, as I have said, characteristic of St. Paul, that when he has once used an antithetical expression of this kind, he recurs to it again and again, and uses it as a nucleus to which fresh connotations attach themselves. And therefore we shall not be surprised, if, in an Epistle written not many months later, the Epistle to the Romans, these words re-appear, with a somewhat amplified reach of meaning. In the second chapter, where he is showing how all, Jew and Gentile alike, had come short of the righteousness of God, he declares that circumcision without obedience is worthless ; and he asks, " If the uncircumcision keep the ordinances of the Law, shall not his uncircumcision be reckoned for circumcision ? And shall not the uncircumcision which is by nature, if it fulfil the Law, judge thee, who with the letter [διὰ γράμματος] and circumcision art a transgressor of the Law?" Here the letter and circumcision seem to stand for the outward religion of form and observance as opposed to the inward religion of obedience. "For," he adds, "he is not a Jew, which is one outwardly ; neither is that circumcision, which is outward in the flesh : but he is a Jew, which is one inwardly ; and circumcision is that of the heart, in the spirit, and not in the letter." It is remarkable that " the letter " here seems to be used as almost exactly equivalent with "the flesh;" St. Paul contrasts circumcision in the flesh with circumcision in the spirit and not in the letter : just as, in Phil. iii. 3, he says, " We are the circumcision, who worship by the Spirit of God, . . . and have no confidence in the flesh." Again, in the seventh chapter of the Epistle to the

Romans, speaking of Christians as being free from the
Law, just as a woman whose husband is dead is free
from the law of her husband and may lawfully be
married to another, he adds, varying the figure after his
usual manner, "Ye also were made dead to the Law
through the Body of Christ; that ye should be joined to
another, even to Him Who was raised from the dead. . . .
For when we were in the flesh, the sinful passions, which
were through the Law, wrought in our members to bring
forth fruit unto death.   But now we have been dis-
charged from the Law, having died to that wherein we
were holden; so that we serve in newness of the Spirit"
—in the new life of which the Spirit is the animating and
inspiring principle,—" and not in oldness of the letter"
—not in the old state of bondage to the Law in which
we were held until, by dying to the Law, we were set
free from it.

In these two passages of the Epistle to the Romans
we seem to recognize a distinct development of meaning
in the words from the first use of them in the Second
Epistle to the Corinthians.   From the first idea of the
written Law as opposed to the free Spirit, they seem to
be taking on the further meaning of the form as opposed
to the essence, the outward as opposed to the inward,
the expression as opposed to the principle.   "Circumcision
is that of the heart, in the spirit, not in the letter:"—
here the original sense of the Spirit, the Giver of life, and
of the written Law which killeth, is still present; but we
see also that it is developing into something further, the
symbol of a yet wider antithesis.   And to serve God in

newness of the spirit and not in oldness of the letter
means more than being no longer under the Law ; it
means the being free from all that formalism, all that
rigid narrowness, of which the Law was the type, and the
rendering to God that reasonable service, that obedience
to the Living Spirit, which is perfect freedom.   Indeed,
something of this kind must have been in St. Paul's mind
when he first used the words in 2 Cor. iii. : for after all
the various antithetical expressions which he there uses
—an epistle written with ink and an epistle written with
the Spirit of the Living God, an epistle on tables of stone
and an epistle on fleshy tables of the heart, the letter
which kills and the spirit which makes alive, the
ministration of death and the ministration of life, the
ministration of condemnation and the ministration of
righteousness, all turning more or less on the same
central idea,—he adds the contrast between that which
passeth away and that which remaineth.   The letter,
then, he connects in thought with τὸ καταργούμενον—the
transitory ; the spirit with τὸ μένον—the permanent.

To dwell at any length upon St. Paul's general use of
the word πνεῦμα would be somewhat beyond our present
scope.   It may be enough to indicate that he uses it first
of the Spirit of God, also called the Spirit of Christ, or
the Holy Spirit, or simply the Spirit ; secondly, of the
spirit of man, the principle which feels, thinks, and
wills, in which sense he sometimes connects it with the
soul, ψυχή, and the body ; and, thirdly, of a power or
influence, the character, manifestations, or results of
which are sometimes defined by qualifying genitives—

as the spirit of meekness, the spirit of faith, the spirit of life, the spirit of adoption, the spirit of power and love and discipline, the spirit of wisdom and revelation. It is also, as we have seen, contrasted with the letter and with the flesh; and it is sometimes used, with a qualifying genitive or clause, in an evil sense—as the spirit of the world, the spirit of bondage, the spirit of slumber, the spirit that worketh in the sons of disobedience. In the use of the word which we have now under consideration the fundamental idea seems to be that of *power*; so that a covenant or dispensation of the spirit will be a system characterized not by method, not by elaborate rule and organization, but by a pervading element of life,—a system in which the processes and functions are mostly invisible,—a system of which our Lord's words hold good, that " the wind bloweth [or the spirit—$\pi\nu\epsilon\hat{\upsilon}\mu\alpha$ —breatheth] where it listeth, and thou hearest the sound thereof, but knowest not whence it cometh and whither it goeth." Perhaps an undesigned testimony to this contrast between the letter and the spirit, as systems respectively of death and of life, may be found in the popular usage which speaks not of the *killing* but of the *dead* letter; as though the letter which kills were itself subject to death, and were incapable of producing any effect without the operation of the life-giving spirit.

And therefore when we speak of the letter and the spirit as respectively the outward and the inward, the form and the essence, the visible and tangible and the invisible and impalpable part of a command or an

institution or an ordinance, we are not really making an
illegitimate use of the words of St. Paul, we are only
developing the latent principle enunciated by him in the
germ, using his terms to express the fuller thought
which has grown out of his pregnant expressions.   Just
as the terms applied by early inquirers are not superseded
but developed into wider connotation by modern science,
so the words of St. Paul are not destroyed but fulfilled
when they are used to express the outgrowth and
development of his own principle.

It is remarkable that the Greek Fathers, to whom
one naturally looks for the interpretation of a Greek
phrase, seem to have quite missed the point of St. Paul's
expression.   Gregory of Nyssa[1] explains the words, "the
letter killeth," as meaning that the Old Testament contains examples of evil deeds, instancing the cases of
David and Bathsheba, and of Hosea taking a wife of
whoredoms.   Origen,[2] with whom the phrase is a familiar
one in connexion with his principle of allegorical interpretation, refers it to the literal and the figurative sense
of Scripture, thus turning it to the disparagement of the
literal as against the mystical sense.   Even Chrysostom[3]
sees no more in it than a statement that the Law enacts

---

[1] "Prœm. in Cantic.," i., p. 470: Πονηρῶν γὰρ ἔχει πραγμάτων
ἐν ἑαυτῷ τὰ ὑποδείγματα.

[2] "Contra Celsum," lib. vi.: Γράμμα τὴν αἰσθητὴν ἐκδοχὴν τῶν
θείων γραμμάτων, πνεῦμα δὲ τὴν νοητήν.

[3] Hom. vi. in II. ad Cor., p. 581: Γράμμα ἐνταῦθα νόμον φησὶ
τὸν κολάζοντα τοὺς πλημμελοῦντας. And so Theophylact, *ad loc.*,
p. 348: Ὁ νόμος ἐὰν λάβῃ τινα ἁμαρτάνοντα κατὰ τὸ δοκοῦν ἐλάχιστον,
ὡς τὸν τὰ ξύλα ἐν σαββάτῳ συλλέξαντα, ἀναιρεῖ.

death as a punishment of transgressors. On the other
hand, Augustine,[1] with that true exegetical instinct which
sets him so high above his contemporaries, at once connects the phrase with St. Paul's words, " Sin, finding
occasion, through the commandment beguiled me, and
through it slew me." He points out that to teach men
how to live soberly, righteously, and godly is but the
letter which killeth, because where no law is there is no
transgression ; that the mere setting before men a high
morality actually places them in a worse position, unless
there be the life-giving Spirit to enable them to live a
new life. He contrasts[2] " the law of the Spirit of life

---

[1] Aug., "De Spiritu et Littera," c. iv.: "Neque enim solo illo
modo intelligendum est quod legimus, 'Littera occidit, spiritus
autem vivificat;' ut aliquid figurate scriptum, cujus est absurda
proprietas, non accipiamus sicut littera sonat, sed aliud quod significat intuentes, interiorem hominem spiritali intelligentia nutri-
amus ; quoniam 'sapere secundam carnem mors est, sapere autem
secundum spiritum vita et pax.' . . . Non ergo solo illo modo
intelligendum est quod ait Apostolus, 'Litera occidit, spiritus
autem vivificat;' sed etiam illo, eoque vel maxime, quo apertissime
alio loco dicit, 'Concupiscentiam nesciebam, nisi lex diceret, Non
concupisces.' Et paulo post ait; 'Occasione accepta peccatum per
mandatum fefellit me, et per illud occidit. . . . Legis littera quæ
docet non esse peccandum, si Spiritus vivificans desit, occidit:
sciri enim facit peccatum potius quam caveri, et ideo magis augeri
quam minui, quia malæ concupiscentiæ etiam prævaricatio legis
accedit." And "Contra Julianum," i. 94: "In hoc est prædesti-
natis adjutorium littera, quia jubendo et non juvando, admonet
infirmos confugere ad spiritum gratiæ. Sic lege legitime utuntur,
quibus bona est, id est, utilis : alioquin per se ipsa littera occidit ;
quia jubendo bonum, et non largiendo caritatem, quæ sola vult
bonum, reos prævaricationis facit."

[2] "Liber de Div. Quæst.," 66 : " Lex peccati dicitur, non quia lex
ipsa peccatum est, sed quia peccatoribus imponitur. Ideo etiam lex

in Christ Jesus" with "the Law of sin and death"—a phrase which he curiously applies to the Law of Moses, —and shows that the latter could at the utmost produce an outward and servile obedience, whereas the former, being written, not on tables of stone, but on fleshy tables of the heart, working not from without but from within, having for its motive not fear but love, is a principle not of death but of life, and sets men free to serve God in newness of the Spirit and not in oldness of the letter.

I have thought it well thus to anticipate an objection which might be made to the subject of these lectures. It might be said that, in using the words "letter" and "spirit" for the outward and inward, the accidental and the essential elements of religious faith and life, we are, in fact, availing ourselves of a popular misapplication of St. Paul's terminology, and sheltering ourselves under his authority while using his words in a perverted sense. Now, it is quite true that sometimes the words of a well-known writer do thus become insensibly deflected into a sense quite alien from their proper meaning. Shakespeare's "One touch of nature makes

---

mortis, quia stipendium peccati mors, aculeus mortis peccatum, virtus autem peccati lex. Peccando enim ad mortem labimur. . . . Lex ergo peccati et mortis, id est, quæ imposita est peccantibus atque morientibus, jubet tantum ne concupiscamus, et tamen concupiscimus. Lex autem spiritus vitæ, quæ pertinet ad gratiam, et liberat a lege peccati et mortis, facit ut non concupiscamus, et impleamus jussa legis, non jam servi legis per timorem, sed amici per caritatem, et servi justitiæ unde illa lex promulgata est." But elsewhere Augustine takes another and a truer view (Serm. clii.): "Illa vero lex peccati et mortis non est lex Dei." He identifies it with the law of sin which is in the members.

the whole world kin "[1] has become a kind of proverb, in
a sense absolutely foreign to the context ; but I maintain
that St. Paul's use, and especially his later use, of the
words "letter" and "spirit" does contain implicitly the
modern application of them, and that in this, as in
other instances, he has, in fact, enriched popular language
by the use of a valuable and pregnant phrase.

For we must not suppose that the distinction between
"letter" and "spirit" goes no deeper than the contrast
between Jewish law and Christian liberty. It is a
distinction which runs through all religion and all
philosophy, and which rests upon a fundamental principle
of human nature—the principle that man is a responsible moral agent, whose highest perfection is not
obedience to an outward law, but fidelity to an inward
spirit. And from this it follows that what he requires
is not a code of rules to be followed implicitly, but
principles of action to be applied by an enlightened
conscience. It is true that in the childhood, as well of
the race as of the individual, there is need of the discipline of the letter—"touch not, taste not, handle not,"
is what children can understand ; but the only value of
such discipline is to produce first a habit of obedience,
and then gradually the deliberate moral choice of those
"who by reason of use have their senses exercised to
discern good and evil." If the dominion of the letter

---

[1] "Troilus and Cressida," Act III., Sc. iii. Delius's note on
this much misunderstood passage is, "Es geht ein und derselbe
natürliche Zug durch die ganze Welt, und bewirkt bei allen Men-
schen, als ob sie verwandt wären, derselben Hang," etc.

is prolonged into mature life, it kills the freedom, the spontaneity, of action. A child may be coerced by a law; a man must be led by the Spirit. The obedience of the letter is valueless in God's sight, because it is mechanical and external; the life of the Spirit is moral, and works from within outwards. It was this principle that underlay our Lord's denunciations of the scribes and Pharisees. They were hypocrites, because their outward acts of religion were not the expression of their inner life; they walked, not after the Spirit, but after the letter. It was this that He meant when He declared that the first and great commandment was the love of God and the second the love of our neighbour, and that on these two commandments hung all the Law and the Prophets. This, too, is what He meant when He told His disciples that it was expedient for them that He should go away, in order that the Comforter might come to them; that the time had come when His personal presence and teaching would be a hindrance to their spiritual growth; that it was time for them to rise above the mechanical obedience of children into the higher and more intelligent life of men; that they needed no longer an outward, but an inward, guide; that they must walk by faith, not by sight. It was this that St. Paul meant when he contrasted the righteousness of the Law with the righteousness of faith, and when he declared that a man is justified by faith, apart from the works of the Law. It was this that, when the mediæval Church had substituted ritual observance and almsgiving for spiritual religion, gave force to Luther's vehement denunciations of the

Papal system, and to his assertion of justification by faith as the *articulus stantis vel cadentis ecclesiæ*—the principle that righteousness, to be of any value, must be, not external, but internal; the result, not of law and discipline, but of the working of the Spirit of God. Every true religious reform, whether within or without the pale of the Christian Church, is in one form or another a re-assertion of the spiritual element—a re-adjustment of the form or letter. Such were those movements in the Church which foreshadowed the Reformation—those of Arnold of Brescia, of the Albigenses, and of the Waldenses, in the twelfth century; of the Brethren and Sisters of the Free Spirit and of the Friends of God in the fourteenth; of John Huss and Jerome of Prague in the fifteenth. Such, too, in its essence, was Buddhism, as a spiritual system, a revolt against the literalisms and formalisms of Brahminism. Such seems to have been the object of the dialectic of Socrates—to detach the minds of his countrymen from formulas, and to open their understandings to receive the spirit of wisdom. And may we not say that the celebrated advice of Dr. Johnson, " Clear your mind from cant," was in effect an admonition to his hearers to shake off the trammels of the letter and to be ready to listen to the spirit of truth, even when its voice sounded contrary to their own prepossessions ?

We recognize the same two elements in the Church in all ages. Always we find in one form or another the Jewish and the Gentile, the dogmatic and the rational element, the tendency to submit to authority and the

tendency to assert the right of private judgment. One
man is never happy until he has an external law to lean
upon; he must be able to refer his actions to some rule
outside himself; he wants an authority which shall
relieve him of the responsibility of deciding for himself.
Another looks, not to an outward law, but to an inward
spirit; he acknowledges the duty of private judgment;
he is not under the Law, but under grace. In morals
you have the man who trusts to system and the man
who trusts to inspiration. In art you have the man
who works by rule and the man who is a law to himself.
In politics you have the man who follows precedent and
the man who trusts to the insight of the moment. Each
character by itself is apt to develop into an extreme:
on the one hand, into a narrow dogmatism, boasting
of its superiority to reason; on the other, into a self-
sufficient rationalism, proud of its independence of all
authority. And it is easier to be wholly in the one
extreme or wholly in the other, to sacrifice reason
altogether or to repudiate authority absolutely, than
to combine the two elements, to temper private judgment with reverence and self-distrust, to blend meekness
with wisdom, and thus to make of twain one new
man. There are not wanting zealots on either side who
will assure you that compromise is impossible; that
between Ultramontanism and Atheism there is no logical
standing-ground; that you must accept everything or
reject everything. In the controversies of the last fifty
years instances of these extremes have not been wanting
in the University. Oxford has produced some of the

foremost assertors of Papal infallibility and some of the most vigorous assailants of all definite belief. Perhaps, when the history of religious thought in the nineteenth century comes to be written, it will be found that the best work of this place has been neither the assertion nor the denial of authority, but the teaching men to look at things as they are, the educating them in the love of truth for its own sake, the impressing on them that they are responsible, not only for what they do, but also for what they believe.

It will be my object in these lectures to discriminate between the letter and the spirit, between the form and the essence, in Scripture exegesis, in the organization and constitution of the Church, in the Sacraments, and in Christian doctrines and ordinances. In doing so, I shall endeavour to be mindful of the objects with which these divinity lecture sermons were founded, prominent among which was "to confirm and establish the Christian faith," and to maintain "the Divine authority of the Holy Scriptures." Hitherto, certainly neither the Christian faith nor the authority of the Scriptures has gained by the persistent maintenance of the letter. Those who from time to time have undertaken the advocacy of the Christian faith have too often made that faith to consist, not in loyalty to the Divine Spirit whereby the whole body of the Church in all ages is governed and sanctified and enlightened, but in a blind adhesion to a formula, an interpretation, a letter. The authority of Scripture has been gravely imperilled when men have invoked it to prove that it was impossible that human beings should

live at the antipodes,[1] that it was impious to believe
that the apparent motion of the sun was due to the
earth's rotation, that geology was a delusive science
because it taught that Creation was the work not of six
days but of untold ages, that witchcraft is a crime
which a Christian State is bound to recognize and to
punish with death, that resistance to even the most
arbitrary government is forbidden to Christian men, that
God for His own greater glory has sent some men into
the world foreordained to eternal damnation.[2]   And, in
the same way, they are not the best defenders of the
Christian faith who refuse to recognize the work of the
Spirit, the Giver of life, in all the manifold varieties of
thought, of organization, of ritual, of character, of social
life, which are evolved in the course of ages, and who
desire to stereotype the Church's life according to the
pattern of the first, or of the fourth, or of the seventh,
or of the sixteenth century.   God is a Spirit ; He cannot
be adequately expressed in terms of human language ;
He dwelleth not in temples made with hands ; no human

---

[1] Augustine, "De Civ. Dei," xvi. c. 9 : "Quod vero et Antipo-
das esse fabulantur, id est, homines a contraria parte terræ, ubi sol
oritur, quando occidit nobis, adversa pedibus nostris calcare vesti-
gia, nulla ratione credendum est. . . Quoniam nullo modo Scriptura
ista mentitur, quæ narratis præteritis facit fidem, eo quod ejus
prædicta complentur: nimisque absurdum est, ut dicatur aliquos
homines ex hac in illam partem, Oceani immensitate trajecta navi-
gare ac pervenire potuisse, ut etiam illic ex uno illo primo homine
genus institueretur humanum."

[2] "Westminster Confession," ch. iii. : "By the decree of God,
for the manifestation of His glory, some men and angels are predes-
tinated unto everlasting life, and others foreordained to everlasting
death."

institutions, however venerable, can contain Him. In the spiritual, as in the natural world, variety is characteristic of His working ; of the one as of the other we may say, " O Lord, how manifold are Thy works ! in wisdom hast Thou made them all."

I trust that to treat of this subject in a reverent spirit and with a sense of responsibility may not be unseasonable at the present time. For, to all appearance, we have entered on a critical period in the history of religious belief. Perhaps it is not so much that new questions are being stirred, as that old questions are assuming an acuter form, and are exciting a wider interest, and are being discussed under new conditions. It is sometimes said that religious questions have lost their interest ; that men no longer care for them. That can hardly be the case, if we may judge from the space which they occupy in the literature of the day. Men do care for them, but they will not accept conventional or traditional solutions of them, they will not defer to mere assertions of authority. At such a time, it is necessary to distinguish very carefully between that which is permanent and essential and that which is temporary and accidental in our religious systems : to endeavour (if I may borrow the words of the Master of Balliol) " to restore the Gospel to its simplicity ; to turn from the letter to the spirit ; to withdraw from the number of the essentials of Christianity points almost too subtle for the naked eye."

The contrast between the letter and the spirit may, perhaps, be not unfitly illustrated by the change which has taken place in this University in the last half century. There are those here who can remember a time when the Academical life of Oxford was compassed about with statutes and formulas and promissory oaths; when every man at his matriculation was obliged to subscribe to the Thirty-nine Articles, and to swear to observe the Laudian Statutes; when, before admission to the foundation of a College or to any statutable office, it was necessary to swear to observe statutes, many of them quite obsolete, with which the candidate was prudently allowed no opportunity of making himself acquainted: when much of the narrowness and exclusiveness of the mediæval system lingered in the modern life of the University. This generation has seen changes such as had not been witnessed certainly since the sixteenth century. Not only has the whole system of obsolete statutes, of vexatious restrictions, of unnecessary oaths been swept away; but new elements, ecclesiastical, social, intellectual, have been freely and ungrudgingly admitted. And I believe that those who are best able to judge will admit that the result has been gain and not loss to the life of the University; that, whereas the letter, the system of antiquated restrictions and exclusions, killed, the spirit, the wider, freer, more modern system of liberty and comprehension has given life. Only let it never be forgotten that the more external restraint is removed, the more need there is of watchful self-restraint; and that if the life of the University is more free and more vigorous than of old, it is so much the more necessary to take care that that life be guided and penetrated by the Spirit of Christ. For remember that the influence of Oxford is no longer confined to a narrow class of society. The life that flows from this place penetrates year by year deeper and deeper into the social system of England; the streams that have their source here affect for good or for evil an ever-widening area. If plain living and high thinking are the rule here, it cannot but affect for good the national life; but if luxury, extravagance, dilettanteism infect Oxford, then, the eye being evil, there is danger lest the whole body be full of darkness.

And you young men who hear me, suffer me to say a word in conclusion specially to you. You are entering upon life at a time when, if religion is to be a factor in your lives at all, it will be necessary for you to make choice between the religion of the letter and the religion of the Spirit. For there is, I fear, in our day a tendency to make religion more and more a matter of system, of compact and definite organization. It is less difficult to be a zealous and enthusiastic Churchman or a zealous and enthusiastic Nonconformist than to be a consistent disciple of Christ; and it is possible to be full of the spirit of Churchmanship or of Nonconformity or of Catholicity or of Protestantism and yet not to have much of the spirit of Christ. For whenever men act together for a common purpose, there is a tendency to lose sight of the end and to think chiefly of the means: and in religious life especially, the visible and tangible is apt to take the place of the invisible and spiritual, and zeal for a Church or for an order or for a party will

sometimes, all unsuspected, become a substitute for zeal
for the Kingdom of God.   But here, too, it is true
that the letter killeth : if we suffer any outward thing,
any organization or form or system, to command our
allegiance and absorb our interest, if we forget that all
these things are but means to an end, and that, apart
from that end, they are in themselves valueless, we are
in the position which St. Paul describes as having begun
in the Spirit and being perfected in the flesh.   The
Kingdom of God does not consist in anything outward,
not in Church government, not in Apostolical succession,
not in Catholic ritual, but in righteousness and peace
and joy in the Holy Spirit.   "It is the Spirit that
quickeneth," says our Lord; "the flesh profiteth nothing :
the words that I speak unto you, they are spirit, and
they are life."   Do not begin with outward things, with
Churchmanship or with party organization or with rules
of conduct.   Begin with the first and great commandment, the love of God, and with the second which is
like unto it, the love of your neighbour : let these be
the supreme motives, the governing force of your life.
If you are looking forward to the Christian ministry as
your work, do not set before you as your first object the
promotion of Church principles or Evangelical principles,
but simply the service of God and of your fellow-men,
and all the rest will fall into its proper place.   Or if you
are purposing to undertake some so-called secular voca-
tion and ministry, then remember that to promote the
well-being of your fellow-men, to cultivate a spirit of
brotherly kindness and helpfulness, to try to bring

together on the ground of their common humanity classes which have learnt to misunderstand and to suspect each other, is a higher and a nobler aim than to serve a political party or to win a political triumph : and that to live after the Spirit, to walk in the Spirit, is the only way in which you can realize the Christian ideal. Christ requires of you, not obedience to an outward rule, not submission to an outward system, but faithfulness to Him. " If ye continue in My word, then are ye My disciples indeed ; and ye shall know the truth, and the truth shall make you free."

LECTURE II.

" Who also made us sufficient as ministers of a New Covenant; not of the letter, but of the spirit: for the letter killeth, but the spirit giveth life."—2 Cor. iii. 6 (R.V.).

I POINTED out in my former lecture that, although the terms " letter " and " Spirit " really cover a much wider area of meaning, yet St. Paul, in his original use of them, does practically identify the letter, γράμμα, the thing written, with the Old Covenant, and the Spirit, the principle of life and freedom, with the New. To St. Paul, indeed, as I have already remarked, the conception of the New Covenant as contained in or dependent on written documents does not seem to have been possible: his sense of the shortness of the time, his expectation of the coming of the Lord, would have made it unnatural for him to contemplate any provision for stereotyping the living Word. The epistle of Christ that he contemplated was written, not with ink, but with the Spirit of the Living God. The permanent record that he cared for was not in tables of stone, but in fleshy tables of the heart. Indeed, human language must of necessity act as a limitation to the freedom of the incomprehensible, illimitable Spirit. "Unspeakable words"—so St. Paul describes what he heard when he was caught up to the third heaven.[1] "Groanings which cannot be uttered"—such are the inarticulate pleadings of the Spirit making intercession for us.[2] As there are "thoughts that lie too deep for tears," so there are thoughts, yearnings, aspirations after God, glimpses of the Eternal, which no words can utter. A man full of the Holy Spirit will strive to pour forth to others the gift which God has committed to him to profit withal : but when he would do this in words, he finds that the more he is possessed with the Spirit the more is he straitened, hampered, baffled by the limitations of speech. He speaks with stammering lips ; his utterances are broken, abrupt, inconsequent. And still more in writing does the mechanical process tend to check and impede the spiritual force ; so that it becomes rough and irregular, like a mountain stream pouring down over a rocky bed. And from this it follows that inspiration—the possession of the spirit of man by the Spirit of God—far from being a guarantee of the adequacy and perfection of his written or spoken utterances, tends rather the other way: it is the un-inspired, shallow, conventional man that puts forth all his mind in a clear, simple, popular style ; the prophet finds the Spirit thwarted by the letter, and he cannot fully utter the truth that is in him. And this we must take into account in dealing with all sacred books. They are sure to be below the level, so to speak, of what

[1] 2 Cor. xii. 4.   [2] Rom. viii. 26.

they record. They do but indicate to us the "depth of
the riches of the wisdom and knowledge of God." They
do but reveal how much there is that cannot be revealed,
"how unsearchable are His judgments, and His ways past
tracing out." They cannot express fully the Mind of the
Spirit. This, too, is why parabolic teaching—the teaching by symbolic act or figurative speech—is so often the
best resource of the highest teachers : because it only
professes to be like a picture shown to children, giving
the mere rudimentary outline of the doctrine, and leaving
it to grow and fructify in the mind of the hearer. And
if the hearer is not himself spiritual, he will not discern
the spirituality of the teaching. And this seems to
have been our Lord's meaning when He said, "Unto
you is given the mystery of the Kingdom of God : but
unto them that are without, all things are done in
parables : that seeing they may see, and not perceive ;
and hearing they may hear, and not understand."
Those who were without, those who were not spiritual
enough to understand the mysteries of the Kingdom of
Heaven, could not get beyond the letter, could not be
taught of the Spirit.

The Old Covenant, then, as contrasted with the New,
was a dispensation of the letter. But although this
was so, and although in the later ages of Jewish history
the reverence for the letter became idolatrous and stifled
the Spirit, yet that the Old Dispensation was in its
essence and inner purpose spiritual, that the Spirit of
God " spake by the Prophets," that the Christian Church
has been guided by a right instinct in adopting the Law

of Moses and the Prophets and the Psalms into her
public services along with the writings of the New
Covenant, will be acknowledged by all who recognize
the continuity of the Divine revelation.

In discussing the letter and the Spirit in the writings
of the Old Testament, it is not necessary to say much as
to the Jewish view of these books, except so far as it has
coloured the Christian view. It has long been clear that
it is impossible to accept the old and simple theory, that
the Jewish acceptance of the Canon guarantees the
authorship and genuineness of the whole. It is impossible to doubt that the historical books are made up of
elements of very varying age and authorship, which have
undergone redaction and arrangement at a comparatively
late period. The most recent theory, that of Well-
hausen, seems to indicate that the earliest legislation
consisted of a very elementary code contained in the
twenty-first, twenty-second, and twenty-third chapters
of Exodus, while the details of the Levitical system were
not fully developed, or at any rate not committed to
writing, till after the time of Ezekiel. We are as yet far
from having arrived at a definite settlement of the
questions connected with the Old Testament ; but should
this theory be received as the final result, it would only
give a still fuller sense to St. Paul's saying that the Law
was spiritual, and would make the Prophetical system
appear as a re-assertion of the simplicity of the earlier
Law.

Nor must we omit to take into account the fact,
that "the reverence which the Jews paid to the letter

of their sacred books as a whole in the time of our Lord,
was in a very great measure a growth of the period
which intervened between the closing of the Old
Testament and the opening of the New."[1] When the
Spirit no longer spake by the Prophets—when the word
of the Lord no longer came to the people fresh and living
and powerful, but only ἐν γράμματι, in the written
documents which the Scribes guarded and interpreted, it
could hardly be but that the letter should take the
place of the Spirit, and that the word of God should
mean to them no longer the living oracles by which He
had manifested Himself to the hearts of His people, but
the dead writings which were all that remained of them.
So it must be always : when faith grows feeble, and the
Living Spirit no longer speaks to the hearts of men, they
must needs fall into the bondage of the letter ; they
must rest upon something outward and tangible—a law,
a writing, an institution, a formula ; when the Law of the
Lord is no longer in men's hearts, they bind it as
phylacteries on their foreheads.

But, as I have said, the question which we have to
consider is, not what was the relation of the Old Testament Scriptures to the Jews, but what is their relation to
us. And this question cannot be settled summarily by
a reference to the views of the early Church. For it
was natural for the first Christians to regard the Jewish
Church with special and even exaggerated reverence.
As I have already pointed out, the Church had no
Scriptures of its own ; the Apostles had been trained in

[1] Myers, " Catholic Thoughts."

the Jewish system ; from children they had known the
Holy Scriptures of the Old Covenant ; and the traditions
of Christ would tell how He was in the habit of referring
to the Law as the standard of truth—" What is written in
the Law ? how readest thou ?"—and how, in the hour of
His temptation, and in His first struggle on the Cross,
the words of Deuteronomy and the Psalms gave expression to His obedience and filial trust.   What, therefore,
could be more natural than that, in their meetings for
worship, Moses and the Prophets and the Psalms should
be used much as they were in the synagogue, and that
the Christian mind should delight to find Christ everywhere in types, and shadows, and mysteries, in the
writings of the Old Covenant ? Even when the destruction of the Temple shattered the organization of the
Jewish Church, still the Jewish Christians remained
faithful to their nationality.   The Gentile converts were
indeed regarded as entering upon the heritage of Israel,
but the Jews were still the old *noblesse;* and the Gentile
came in somewhat as a *parvenu.*   The Gentile entered
the Church stripped of all his past religious life : the
gods of Olympus were no gods ; or worse, they were
demons whom Christ had come to drive out : but the
Jew came in clothed in all the majesty of his past
history, the adoption, and the glory, and the covenants,
and the giving of the Law, and the service of God, and
the promises.   And so it was inevitable that the traditions of the primitive Church should be Jewish ; that
the infant Church should be wrapped in Jewish swaddling
clothes.   " To the Jew first, and also to the Gentile " was

St. Paul's own rule. But gradually the Gentile element became stronger ; gradually, too, Apostolic writings, addressed originally to particular Churches, passed from city to city, and became the common property of all ; gradually oral traditions, derived from those who from the beginning were eye-witnesses and ministers of the Word, took shape in written documents, compiled by men who had traced the course of all things accurately from the first : and the Church, already inheriting from the synagogue the traditional reverence for the Canon of the Old Testament, transferred an equal share of that reverence to the gradually accumulating writings of the New Covenant, and the two literatures were fused into one,[1] and the Law and the Prophets were read with the Gospels and Epistles, and the Psalms of David were sung in the assemblies along with Christian hymns, and a new light was shed back upon the old writings, and the mysteries of the faith were found embedded deep in the books of the Old Testament. The two streams flowed on for a time, like the Arve and the Rhone, distinct in colour, the one turbid after its long course from Mount Sinai, the other limpid and fresh from the Galilean lake ; but little by little they mingled and became one, and the Catholic Church flowed on, to receive new elements, to water new lands, to make glad the city of God.

It is necessary to remember the way in which the Jews had come to regard their sacred books, in order to

---

[1] Tertullian de Præscr., 36 : " (Ecclesia) legem et prophetas cum evangelicis et apostolicis litteris miscet et inde potat fidem."

understand the tradition which the Christian Church inherited on the subject of Inspiration. Scarcely anything is said of inspiration in the New Testament beyond the well-known phrase in 2 Tim. iii., γραφὴ θεόπνευστος; nor does it appear that any kind of formal definition was attempted by early writers. The Christian Scriptures fell naturally into the same rank with the Jewish, and were described in the same terms. And so it came about, that the Old and the New Testament were regarded by the Church as of co-ordinate authority, and the Old Testament was used as freely and unhesitatingly as the New in proof of Christian doctrine. Origen, indeed, rests the proof of the inspiration of the Old Testament on the authority of Christ, thus making the Old subordinate to and dependent on the New ; but generally the Jewish Scriptures were received without question and without any particular theory as a part of the Divine revelation, as part of the vineyard which had been taken away from the original husbandmen and given to the Christian Church.

It appears then, that, setting aside such passing extravagances as those of Marcion and the early Gnostics, the Old Testament was from the first adopted into the Christian Canon, was indeed for a time the only sacred literature of the Church, and was regarded afterwards with the same reverence as the New. It would seem that at the Reformation there must have been a tendency to reject or at any rate to depreciate the Old Testament, for the original form of the seventh Article of the Church of England ran thus : "The Old Testa-

ment is not to be put away, as though it were contrary
to the New, but to be kept still." And the nineteenth
Article, as it stood in 1552, indicates a tendency to exalt
the spirit at the expense of the letter; for it runs, "They
are not to be hearkened unto who affirm that Holy
Scripture is given only to the weak, and do boast themselves continually of the Spirit, of Whom (they say)
they have learned such things as they teach, although
the same be most evidently repugnant to the Holy
Scripture." But this tendency, if it existed, soon passed
away, and the effect of the Reformation was undoubtedly
to enforce upon the Protestant Churches stricter views of
the inspiration of Scripture. When men's faith in an
infallible Church was shaken, it became necessary to
substitute some other foundation for the Catholic faith
to rest on, and the infallibility of Scripture took the
place of the infallibility of the Church. So that, until
of late years, the alternative was to accept the Bible as
a whole, as from beginning to end the direct utterance
of the Holy Spirit, as thus guaranteed against error and
imperfection of whatever kind, and as equally perfect
and equally valuable in all its parts; or, on the other
hand, to reject it as a fiction, unworthy of the serious
attention of reasonable men. To us, the subject presents
itself under an entirely different aspect. For we have
learnt to lay aside preconceived theories, and to start
from the Bible as it stands, to compare it with the
sacred books of other religions, to study it in the light
of history, to inquire into its influence on human
character and progress, to recognize in it a human

D

literature, and to ask, Does or does not this high
morality, this deep insight into human nature, this
unique power of stirring the human heart, compel us to
ascribe to writings so immeasurably in advance of the
age and nation in which they appeared a more than
human origin ? We have learnt to distrust the theory
of a mechanical inspiration, such as, for example, that
which describes the Spirit breathing into the prophets
as a flute-player into a flute ; [1] and to regard the Divine
inspiration, not as something apart or isolated, a process
beginning and ending in the production of a book, but
as the pouring out of God's Spirit upon all flesh, as the
putting His laws into men's hearts and writing them
upon their minds.   We have learnt that, as in the case
of Israel, so in the case of the Christian Church, the
living society existed before the written books ; and that
the books are the outcome and the record of the spiritual
life penetrating and permeating the society.   And therefore upon us there seems to be laid the task of en-
deavouring gradually to discriminate between the essential and the accidental, between the temporary and
permanent elements in the sacred writings.   And with
regard especially to the Old Testament, we have to face the
very grave question, What are the relations in which the
Hebrew Scriptures stand to the modern Christian Church ?

In the recently published " Life of Lord Shaftesbury,"
we are told that that excellent man was shocked by the
assertion that the Books of Chronicles and the Gospel of
St. Luke did not stand on the same ground of inspiration;

---

[1] Ὡσεὶ αὐλητὴς αὐλὸν ἐμπνεύσας.—Athenagoras.

and that he maintained that, "there is no security whatever except in standing upon the faith of our fathers,
and saying that the blessed old Book is ' God's word
written,' from the very first syllable to the very last,
and from the last back to the first." [1] That was a view
which was common enough formerly, but which few
probably even moderately educated persons hold now.
On the other hand, there are some who desire Christianity
without Judaism ; who think that the Church has outgrown her early wrappings, and that the Old Testament
books have for us a purely historical or literary interest. [2]
But it is impossible for the Christian faith to sever itself
from its antecedents ; the genealogies contained in two
of our Gospels, whatever may be the difficulties connected with them, may at least stand for symbols of the
fact that Christ came of the Jewish race as concerning
the flesh ; and if there is such a thing as a science
of religion, it teaches us not the independence but the
continuity and solidarity of all religious systems.
Christ, in speaking to the Jews, seems to make the
belief of Moses' writings an antecedent condition to the
belief of His words ; and though we do not, like them,
accept Christ on the testimony of Moses, yet, in a wider
sense, the Law—not merely the Law of Moses, but the
whole system of discipline, of prohibition, of repression,
which that Law embodies—has its place in the work of
bringing us to Christ. But, at the same time, this age
is becoming more alive to the fact that there are in

[1] " Lord Shaftesbury's Life," iii., p. 7.
[2] *E.g.* Schleiermacher, " Glaubenslehre," ii., § 131.

Christianity other and perhaps not less important
elements than the Jewish. It was, as I have said, quite
natural for the early Church *consecrare origines suas* by
looking back to the glories of the Old Covenant, softened
as to its less attractive features by the haze of antiquity;
but, as time went on, other threads became interwoven
in the fabric of the Christian tradition, and fresh tints
were introduced ; the Gentile element tended more and
more to prevail over the Jewish, and the seamless robe,
not yet completed, contains in its texture the work of
many ages and of many lands. It is, indeed, quite true
that in one aspect Christianity is an outgrowth of
Judaism. But it is easy to assign too much importance
to the Judaic element in it. For though Christ was
called the Son of David, though He was descended from
Jewish ancestors and brought up amid Jewish surroundings, yet he was in a far truer and more characteristic
sense the Son of Man : there was in Him nothing distinctively Galilean, nothing essentially Jewish ; He was
not of one age nor of one nation, but of all. And the
Christian faith, though springing out of Jewish soil and
having its roots deeply entwined in the ancient Jewish
Scriptures, has drawn the elements of its growth not
only from its roots but also from the atmosphere into
which it has pushed its branches ; the grain of mustard
seed which Christ planted has grown into what it is
under the joint action of Oriental and Greek and Latin
and Teutonic influences.

It appears probable, therefore, that in the Christianity
of the future the position of the Old Testament will be

somewhat less prominent, less directly authoritative, than it has been in the past. The oldness of the letter will give place to the newness of the spirit. The Old Covenant, indeed, can never lose its importance in any complete system of theology. But there will be less tendency to dwell upon minute points; less attention will be given to the letter of Messianic anticipations, and more to the spirit of hope and yearning for a better future which pervades the whole. To take an instance: St. Peter, in asserting the impossibility of Christ's being holden of death, applies to His Resurrection the words of Psa. xvi.: "I have set the Lord always before me; because He is at my right hand, I shall not be moved. Therefore my heart is glad, and my glory rejoiceth: my flesh also shall dwell in safety. For Thou wilt not leave my soul to Sheol; neither wilt Thou suffer Thine holy one to see corruption. Thou wilt show me the path of life: in Thy presence is fulness of joy." We cannot doubt that the letter of this Psalm refers to the feelings, the joys and sorrows, of the Psalmist himself, and expresses his own confident expectation that God, Whom he saw always before him, would not leave him finally in the pit of trouble, but would at length raise him up and make him glad with the joy of His countenance. But St. Peter adds his own comment, to the effect that David both died and was buried, and therefore he could not be speaking of himself; but that, being a Prophet, "and knowing that God had sworn with an oath to him, that of the fruit of his loins He would set one upon his throne; he foreseeing this spake of the Resurrection of

the Christ, that neither was He left in Hades, nor did His
Flesh see corruption." But we need not, surely, hold that
David in any literal sense foresaw the Resurrection of the
Christ Who should come after him; rather in the confidence which he expresses is involved the everlasting
principle that God will never leave any of His faithful
servants to perish utterly; that in His time He will
deliver them from the pit of corruption. And from this
it will follow, for those who believe in Christ, that for
Him above all it was impossible that He should be
holden of the pains of death; that God was pledged by
His righteousness to deliver Him. And so, when we
use this Psalm on Easter morning or the fifty-third
chapter of Isaiah on Good Friday, we need not dwell
upon supposed literal anticipations of the Passion or
Resurrection, but we may think of Christ as the Son of
Man, gathering up into Himself all the sorrows and all
the hopes and all the longings of humanity, and fulfilling them by giving them for all future ages a wider
and a nobler meaning than Psalmists and Prophets had
ever foreseen. If, indeed, we are to seek in the Old
Testament chiefly for literal and, so to say, mechanical
anticipations of future events, it loses most of its value
and interest for ordinary persons, and becomes a curious
study for ingenious interpreters: but if we will be content to see in it a record of God's Spirit working upon
the spirit of man, teaching him first the simplest and
most rudimentary lessons, then leading him up to higher
truth, and finally bidding him look forward to the
maturity of spiritual manhood, when the outward Law

should have done its work, and when God would put His
law in their inward parts, and write it on their hearts ;—
if we will be content so to regard the Old Testament, we
shall find that Moses in the Law and the Prophets did
write of Jesus of Nazareth, for that the things which
prophets and kings desired to see are manifested in Him,
and that the grace of Christ which was latent in the Old
Testament is revealed in the New.[1]

The principle which is here asserted, of the inferiority
of the letter to the spirit, has one special aspect which
formed the subject of an entire course of Bampton
Lectures[2] more than sixty years ago, but which it is
impossible not to touch upon briefly, I mean the allegorical interpretation of Scripture. "The letter killeth,
but the spirit giveth life," was a favourite text with
Origen, who is commonly regarded as the father of
mystical interpretation.   Not, indeed, that this system of interpretation originated with Origen ; we must
go much further back to find its source. It must
be borne in mind that the Old Testament was to the
Jews the whole of their literature ; all that we find in
past history, in the thoughts of poets and philosophers

---

[1] Aug., Quæst. in Exod., ii. 73 : "Ad vetus Testamentum timor
potius pertinet, sicut ad novum dilectio: quamquam et in vetere
novum lateat, et in novo vetus pateat."   And Serm. clx.: "Novum
Testamentum in veteri velabatur: vetus Testamentum in novo
revelatur."   Augustine points out that we do wrong to the New
Testament if we place it in the same rank with the Old : "Sicut
veteri testamento, si esse ex Deo bono et summo negetur; ita et
novo fit injuria, si veteri æquetur."

[2] Conybeare's Bampton Lectures on the "History of Allegorical
Interpretation," 1824.

of all ages and of all countries, they found in Moses and the Prophets and the Psalms. And therefore it was quite natural that their ideas should clothe themselves in Old Testament language ; that they should see, in the Old Testament, types where we might see only coincidences ; that they should say, " All this was done that it might be fulfilled which was spoken by the Prophet," where we should at the utmost give point to a narrative by a passing allusion. For example, when St. Matthew, writing to Jews and from a Jewish point of view, mentions that the Infant Messiah was taken into Egypt for refuge during Herod's life, where we should have perhaps alluded to the ancient connexion of Israel with Egypt, he says that the sojourning in Egypt took place in order " that it might be fulfilled which was spoken of the Lord by the Prophet, saying, Out of Egypt have I called My Son." [1] St. Paul, again, when he wishes to connect the spiritual life of Israel in the past with the Messiah Who was his life, refers to a Jewish legend which related how in the wilderness a rock followed the people in their wanderings and supplied them with water, and adds, " That Rock was Christ." [2] When he wishes to contrast the spiritual freedom of Christians with the bondage of the Law, he thinks of the two sons of Abraham, the one by a bondmaid, the other by a free woman, and he says, " these things are an allegory ; for these are the two Covenants." [3] And from these it was an easy and a natural step to find beneath the surface of the sacred writings inexhaustible mines of spiritual

---

[1] Matt. ii. 15.　　　　[2] 1 Cor. x. 4.　　　　[3] Gal. iv. 24.

truth which only needed to be explored by those who
had the skill and insight to search them out. St. Paul's
hint that the natural man could not receive the things
of the Spirit of God,[1] was taken to mean that, while the
letter of Scripture was apparently plain, it required a
special initiation to reach that which alone was valuable,
the spiritual or mystical sense. And this tendency to
spiritualize and allegorize, which we find thoroughly
established by the second century of the Christian era,
was greatly encouraged by the circumstances of the
time. The policy of Alexander the Great in settling a
large colony of Jews in his newly founded city of Alexandria had brought the Jewish mind for the first time
into contact with Greek philosophy and speculation.
The effect of this had been twofold. On the one hand,
a certain number of Jews had forsaken the traditions of
their fathers and had broken altogether with the Mosaic
law ; and, on the other hand, many, without abandoning
the religion of Israel, had become disciples and students
of the Platonic philosophy. But then it followed that
if the Greek philosophy was true and the Old Testament Scriptures contained all wisdom, the one must be
implicitly contained in the other ; and thus Philo, the
representative of Alexandrian Judaism, endeavoured
"to accommodate the Mosaic history to an incredulous
age, and to blend Judaism and Platonism into one har-
monious system."[2] The allegorical method of interpretation was not indeed invented by Philo ; but it was by
him that it was elaborated and popularized, and it was

[1] 1 Cor. ii. 14.   [2] Milman, "History of Christianity," i. 25.

mainly through his influence that it passed into the
Christian Church. In Origen, who was a disciple of
Clement of Alexandria, the system found its fullest
development. His fundamental principle is, "The letter
killeth, but the spirit giveth life." But in carrying out
this principle he virtually killed the letter by turning it
into a cryptograph, the literal meaning of which was
unimportant or even misleading. By disparaging the
literal and exalting the spiritual sense, he opened a door
to sublimating the whole of Scripture into a mystical
sense, intelligible only to the initiated, and so turning
it into a book of riddles, of which the key was in the
hands of the wise. To St. Augustine, and doubtless to
others like-minded with him, the allegorical interpretation of the Old Testament was welcome as enabling
him to get over difficulties in the literal sense which had
troubled him when feeling his way towards a belief in
Christianity.[1] Indeed, St. Augustine, though his powerful common sense saved him from much of the extravagance of some both earlier and later interpreters, and
though he never evacuates the literal sense, yet at the
same time allows himself in the widest latitude of allegorical interpretations, especially in his favourite subject
of mystical numbers. For example :[2] Moses, Elijah,
and our Lord each fasted forty days. This number he
expounds thus : Four is the number of time ; the day

---

[1] Aug., "Conf.," vi. c. 4.: "Sæpe in popularibus sermonibus suis
dicentem Ambrosium lætus audiebam : 'Litera occidit, spiritus
autem vivificat;' cum ea, quæ ad literam perversitatem docere
videbantur, remoto mystico vetamento spiritaliter aperiret."

[2] Aug., "De Doct. Christ.," ii. c. 16.

and the year being each divided into four parts. Ten
signifies the Creator and the creature; three being the
Trinity; seven the creature, being made up of three,
the heart and soul and mind with which we are to love
God, and four, the elements of which the body is composed. Thus the Law, the Prophets, and the Gospel
unite in bidding us to keep the mystic forty days by
fasting from the things of time and subjecting body and
soul to God Who made them. Again,[1] in the hundred
and fifty and three great fishes caught on the right side
of the ship in the second draught of fishes, Augustine
finds a great mystery. Ten is the number of the commandments of the Law, seven of the gifts of the Spirit.
Thus seventeen signifies the Old and the New Dispensation. But if we make an arithmetical progression
beginning with 1 and ending with 17, we arrive at 153,
which therefore signifies the great multitude which no
man can number, saved under the Law and the Gospel,
who shall be on the right side of the Judge. He has
also another and a far more elaborate and intricate
exposition of the same number, which it would be
tedious to set forth here.[2]

[1] Aug., "Enarr. in Psa. xlix."
[2] Aug., "De Diversis Quæs.," lvii., and in " Joh. Ev.," Tractat.
cxxii. In the narrative in St. John vi., where the disciples are
related to have rowed five and twenty or thirty furlongs before
Jesus came to them, we find these numbers elaborately allegorized
thus :—25 is the product of 5 × 5. He refers this to the 5
books of Moses, the 5 porches at Bethesda, the 5 loaves which fed
5000 men. From this he deduces that 25 = the Law. But the
Law was imperfect, therefore it is perfected in 6: for God made
the world in 6 days. So 5 × 6 = 30, that the Law may be fulfilled in the Gospel, and Jesus comes to those who fulfil the Law.

Probably the most familiar and the most complete example of the allegorical interpretation of Scripture is to be found in the "Magna Moralia" of St. Gregory. This work consists in an elaborate exposition of the Book of Job, in which the whole book is violently Christianized, and the minutest detail is pressed into the service of the Gospel. Thus the seven sons of Job signify the twelve Apostles, for the product of four and three, which are the parts of seven, is twelve. Elsewhere the seven sons are the seven gifts of the Holy Spirit, and the three daughters are the Christian graces of Faith, Hope, and Charity. The oxen which were plowing and the asses feeding beside them when the Sabæans fell upon them represent—the oxen, the more perfect Christians who do the work ; the asses, the simpler brethren who feed in green pastures. In the end of the book, Job had double the number of sheep and camels and oxen and she asses restored to him that he had possessed at first, but only the same number of sons and daughters ; which signifies that his original sons and daughters were living in the unseen world, so that in fact he had double of all. The camel signifies the Redeemer, because He stoops to bear our burdens ; and hence the camel going through the eye of the needle means Christ going through the narrow gate of death.

I have touched upon these curiosities of Christian literature, not only because they illustrate a strange and formerly important aspect of my subject, but also because the allegorical system of interpretation is not unheard of in our day. It was strenuously vindicated in the last

but one of the " Tracts of the Times," by one whose name
can never be spoken in this place without honour and
reverence—John Keble, who was bold enough to select
for defence two of the most astonishing instances from
the so-called Epistle of Barnabas. The author of this
work wished to show how circumcision is to be spiritually understood. " See," he says, " how Abraham, who
first gave circumcision, looked forward to Jesus. He
circumcised the men of his household, in number 318.
Of the two letters which in the Greek numerals stand
for 18, 10 is represented by I, and 8 by H. Here, thou
hast Ἰησοῦς. 300 is represented by T. And T is the
figure of the Cross. He therefore sets forth Jesus by
two letters and the Cross by one." It is obvious to
remark that this depends on the Greek numerals, and,
that in the Hebrew there is no such signification ; and
further, that 318 was the number of Abraham's household, not at the time of circumcision, but long before, in
the war with Chedorlaomer. This is explained by the
theory that the mystery of the number was wonderfully
revealed to Abraham, and that his household was pro-
videntially kept to the same number. The same epistle
finds in the words of the first Psalm, " He shall be like a
tree planted by the streams of water," in the tree the
Cross, in the water Christian Baptism.

It is, perhaps, enough to remark, that such a system
of interpreting Scripture would require inspired interpreters. If the Bible means all this, plain men and
women cannot hope to understand it. A system which
makes Scripture mean anything is likely to end in

making it mean nothing. Sermons constructed on this principle—and such have been preached in the Church of England in our day—could hardly touch any human heart. When a man of learning and reputation finds in the words, "I have determined to winter at Nicopolis" our Lord's determination to leave the eternal spring of heaven and to winter in this cold, bleak, snowy world; and in Nicopolis, the city of victory, an indication of His victory over evil—"Notice the junction of the two: the winter and the success:"—there is nothing more to be said.[1]

But we must not suffer the frivolities of interpreters to turn us aside from the serious study of the Old Testament. We may well acknowledge a typical character in it, wherever there is any real analogy discernible: as, for example, when Esau and Jacob are used as illustrations of different types of character, or when God's dealings with Israel are taken as indications

---

[1] "Sermons preached in a Religious House," by Dr. John Mason Neale; vol. i., serm. xv. An equally astonishing instance is to be found in the same volume, serm. xiii., on the text 1 Sam. xxiii. 20—"Now therefore, O King, come down according to all the desire of thy soul to come down." The literal sense of the passage, which is a petition of the Ziphites to Saul to come down that they may deliver David into his hand, is nowhere alluded to. It is applied to Christ's coming down, first in His Incarnation, "from the crown of celestial majesty to the Diadem of Thorns; from the seat on the Right Hand of the Father to the Cross on the right hand of the impenitent thief;" and, secondly, to His coming down in the Eucharist. "What better, what dearer prayer, as we first, in each celebration, kneel before the Altar, than this—'Now therefore, O King, come down according to all the desire of Thy soul to come down'?"

of His method of dealing with nations. We need not
hesitate to apply to ourselves the utterances of Psalmists
and Prophets, so far as they turn, not on local or temporary accidents, but on eternal principles. We must
endeavour to study Scripture seriously, not as a book containing a secret meaning accessible only to the initiated,
not as an oracle skilfully arranged to convey different
senses to different inquirers, but as a collection of writings,
the interpretation of which depends greatly on the circumstances and the age of their composition. Cardinal
Newman indeed, in the last work that he wrote in the
Church of England, says that "it may almost be laid
down as an historical fact, that the mystical interpretation and orthodoxy will stand or fall together." One is
encouraged to hope that the case may not be so bad, by
noticing the kind of instances that he quotes as specimens
of his rule—the mention of "waters" in the Apocalypse
in support of the mixture of water and wine in the
Eucharist ; "We went through fire and water, and
thou broughtest us out into a wealthy place," as an
argument for purgatory; "My heart is inditing of a
good matter," or "has burst forth with a good Word,"
as a proof of our Lord's Divinity. One hopes, I say,
that orthodoxy does not depend on an exegesis of this
kind ; but in any case, ὅσιον προτιμᾷν τὴν ἀλήθειαν—we
must prefer truth even to orthodoxy. To find a proof
of purgatory in a poetical reference to fire in a Hebrew
Psalm is ingenious indeed, but, to ordinary minds, not
convincing. Indeed, it would be possible, if it were not
profane, to construct on this method a system of Scrip-

tural proofs of the most heterodox doctrines. We cannot doubt that Luther's manly common sense hit the mark when he declared that the literal sense of Scripture alone contains the whole essence of faith and of Christian theology; and that we must aim at obtaining " unum, simplicem, et certum sensum literalem."

Here, too, lies the danger of what is commonly called the devotional study of the Scriptures. Nothing can be better, nothing more edifying, than to take what we may call the more inward parts of Scripture, pre-eminently the Psalms, and to make them the basis of religious meditations, so long as those meditations do not become morbid or fanciful; but if we yield to the temptation to seek for edification everywhere alike, we shall be likely to run into a feeble mysticism, and to turn Scripture into something quite different from what it really is.

And yet we cannot doubt that even the unintelligent, even the superstitious, use of Scripture has been of vast spiritual benefit to untold numbers of simple Christians. Not only in the Gospels and Epistles of the New Testament, not only in the Psalms, but in the historical and sapiential and prophetical literature of the Old Testament, have pious souls sought and found the nourishment of their spiritual life. How much of what is best in the English character, how much of its sturdy persistency, how much of its love of honesty and plain dealing, how much of its reverence for domestic purity, may be traced to the familiarity of our forefathers with the letter of the Old Testament! How much do we owe to that element of rugged Puritanism, which was built

up mainly from Hebrew materials! And if we have
outgrown the narrowness of Puritanism, let us not
think that we have also outgrown the Old Testament.
The letter killeth—true : but as in the education of the
race so in that of the individual, we need the stern
assertion of a moral standard, even though it be an
imperfect, a rudimentary one, to make us dissatisfied
with ourselves, to force upon us the contrast between
what we are and what we ought to be, to be to us a
παιδαγωγὸς εἰς Χριστόν, even though we may shrink and
struggle against being led to Him. In some sense we
still need that the letter should kill ; for not till we have
learnt to say with St. Paul, " O wretched man that I am!
who shall deliver me from the body of this death ? "
can we say with the same Apostle, " The law of the
Spirit of life in Christ Jesus hath made me free from the
law of sin and death."

ADDITIONAL NOTE TO LECTURE II.

It may perhaps be not uninstructive to see into what strange
conceptions of God's nature even good men have been led by
dwelling too much upon the letter of Scripture. The following
passage is from "Occasional Sermons," by the Rev. C. Clayton, of
Cambridge, p. 80 : "'They will rise to shame and everlasting contempt.' In the midst of their cries for deliverance the righteous
Lord will 'laugh' at their calamities. While in their fear they
will be calling on the mountains to fall upon them and the hills
to cover them, He will 'mock' at their distress. Only think,
brethren, think of that! The loving Saviour, who once shed His
Blood for their sins, 'laughing' and 'mocking' the impenitent at a
season when most of all they will need a friend!"

This, however, is weak compared with the following, from the
sermons of John Cawood, of Bewdley, a preacher of some reputation in his day (vol. i., p. 239) : "The wicked in Hell will have

E

bodies fitted to endure everlasting burnings; bodies exquisitely sensible of the smallest pain, and immortally strong to endure the greatest; every part of their body will be most tender to feel, and every feeling part will be filled with agony. For their bodies will be 'vessels of wrath fitted for destruction;' vessels filled to the brim with fire, and fitted to endure this fire for ever. . . . Nor will sinners in Hell have one drop of water to cool their tongue, or to quench their thirst; streams of fiery brimstone will be their only portion to drink. . . . Painful as it is, even in imagination, to dwell on these inextinguishable fires, flashing, and raging, and roaring above, beneath, and all around; yet must we proceed in this painful course, for the suffering of the lost is not half told. . . . After the wicked have suffered for millions of millions of millions of ages, there will still be an eternity of suffering to come. . . . Who can tell the grains of dust in the globe of the earth? Who can count the drops of water in the sea? Who can number the stars of light in the heaven? Add these grains of dust to these drops of the ocean, and multiply the sum by the stars of night, and the vast amount overwhelms the mind. But when the wicked in hell shall have been tormented through millions of ages equal to this mighty amount, there will still be an eternity of torment to come. O eternity, eternity! . . . Eternity is a circle, whose centre is everywhere, whose circumference is nowhere. Every moment will the wicked suffer eternal pain, and suffer it through eternity. Were an angel to write figures on the sky from pole to pole, until the whole sky was blackened with figures; yet when the wicked shall have been tormented in hell as many years as would in figures blacken the whole sky, still would there be an eternity of torment to come." An attempt is made to express the same idea by a different image, in a German treatise—Suso, Büchlein von der Weisheit, c. xi., von immerwährendem Weh der Hölle: "Wir begehrten (sagen die Verdammten) nichts anderes, denn wäre ein Mühlstein so breit als alles Erdreich, und um sich so gross, dass en den Himmel allenthalben berührte, und käme ein kleines Vöglein je über hunderttausend Jahre und bisse ab dem Stein so gross, als der zehnte Theil ist eines Hirskörnleins, und aber über hunderttausend Jahre so viel, als dass es in zehnhunderttausend Jahren so viel ab dem Stein klaubte, als gross ein Hirskörnlein ist: wir Armen begehrten nichts anderes, denn, so des Steines ein Ende wäre, dass auch dann unsere Marter ein Ende hätte; und das mag nicht sein!"

LECTURE III.

"The letter killeth, but the spirit giveth life."—2 COR. iii. 6.

IN speaking of the letter and the spirit in connexion with the Bible, we must try to divest ourselves of vague traditional notions, and to look at the facts as they are. And it is of the first importance to remember that the books which we now call by a single name came into being under the utmost variety of outward circumstances, widely separated from each other in age, in the culture of their authors, in the religious conditions which called them forth. Of the Old Testament books, indeed, we know scarcely anything as to their origin except what we can gather from internal indications : the Prophets for the most part tell their own tale : the Book of Job stands rugged and solitary, like an erratic block that has found its way from some far-off mountainside into the midst of surroundings of a wholly different age and character : the Psalms are a collection of gems, representing various conditions of religious sentiment, some sparkling with joy and gladness, some darkened with sorrow and penitence, but all reflecting the ex-

perience of human life and the feelings of human
hearts : Ecclesiastes gives us the picture of a human
soul, " feeling its way through a night of darkness to
some measure at least of light and knowledge." [1]
But in the case of the New Testament all this is
reversed. Whatever doubts may beset the authorship of
certain Gospels or Epistles, the general origin of the
Canon is quite clear. We see that it sprang up in a
quite informal way, and in answer to the requirements
of the infant Church. St. Paul hears of irregularities
which required repression in one Church ; of forgetful-
ness of his teaching in another ; or he feels impelled to
write to a Church that he had never seen, and to impart
to them some spiritual gift ; or he has to send back a
runaway slave to his master, and he writes a letter to
tell him of the new relation in which his slave stands to
him as a Christian brother; or a Christian of intelligence
and education, wishing to assure a young friend of the
certainty of the things in which he had been instructed,
writes a detailed statement of the result of his observa-
tions and inquiries. And the books which we possess
are but survivors, we may well believe the fittest, but
still only survivors, of others of which we know nothing.
St. Paul's earliest Epistle to the Corinthians, the many
declarations of the Gospel narrative which St. Luke says
were drawn up before he wrote—these and doubtless
other writings have perished. How entirely does this
informal—we might be tempted to say fortuitous, but
that we may be sure that God's never-failing providence

[1] Cf. Bradley's " Lectures on Ecclesiastes."

ordered it—how entirely does this informal growth of
a sacred literature contrast with the orderly and systematic elaboration of a religious formula, such as we
should frame if it were our purpose to found a Church
or an order ! Indeed, one is apt to suspect that the
popular notion of the Bible as a single and systematic
handbook of religion has sprung up very much from
men's preconceived notions of what such a book ought
to be, rather than from any thoughtful consideration of
what it actually is. Compare the Bible, for instance,
with the Koran. In one sense, no doubt, the Koran is
the more unsystematic of the two, for its component
parts have been hopelessly dislocated, so that it is
inconsecutive in the highest degree. But still there is
no variety, no light and shade, as in the Bible : it is the
work of a single author ; uniform and without relief,
like an Arabian desert. The characteristic feature of
the Bible is its perfectly human tone, so that it seems
incredible that it should have been forced and strained
into a mere handbook of religion. And this suggests a
further thought about the Bible—that it is not so much
an inspired book as the writing of inspired men. It
would not be within the scope of this lecture to enter
upon a discussion of the nature and limits of inspiration:
but as our subject is the letter and the spirit, it is not
out of place to point out that the letter of the Bible is
the result of the working of the Holy Spirit of God,
not superseding the human consciousness, not destroying
the writer's individuality, but elevating and pervading
it, so that a man, being full of the Holy Spirit which is

given him to profit withal, gives forth that which he has received, ministers the gift to others, as a good steward of the manifold grace of God.

Probably the view of the primitive Church on the subject of inspiration may be summed up in St. Paul's words, " To one is given through the Spirit the words of wisdom ; and to another the word of knowledge, according to the same Spirit : to another faith, in the same Spirit ; and to another gifts of healings, in the one Spirit ; and to another workings of miracles ; and to another prophecy : . . . but all these worketh the one and the same Spirit, dividing to each one severally even as He will." [1]   There is no trace of a belief in any separate and independent form of inspiration for the writing of sacred books : the wisdom and the Spirit with which the Apostles spake would be the same wisdom and the same Spirit with which they wrote.

If indeed there exists an opposition between the spirit and the letter ; if, as I tried to show in my last lecture, the mere fact of reducing to writing the utterances of the free Spirit must tend to confine and hamper them ; then inspiration in the highest sense, far from being limited to written documents, would rather be independent of them. The letter is the record of the mind of men who were, as we believe, filled with the Spirit ; and we need not doubt that God's providence watched over the record, and that He, without Whom not a sparrow falls to the ground, cared for the future of His Church ; but the letter cannot take the place of

[1] 1 Cor. xii. 8–11 (R.V.).

the Living and Life-giving Spirit. The tendency of the exaltation of the Bible into the position of God's final utterance to His Church has been to weaken the belief in the constant presence of the Divine Spirit, in the unceasing inspiration by which He is still leading men into all the truth. If we think that when the Canon of the New Testament was closed, God's voice ceased to be heard, the Scripture itself will be to us no longer an utterance of the Living Word but a dead idol; it will lead men to fall back upon the life of the first century instead of believing that God has never ceased to manifest Himself in an ever-widening revelation through all the varied life and thought and knowledge of the succeeding ages.

It seems clear that we should approach Scripture in a manner corresponding with its genesis. If it had been a formal treatise, supernaturally drawn up to serve as a text-book of religion, it would be reasonable that we should use it as a text-book, accepting it in the letter as scientifically accurate, making no distinction between its parts, appealing to a single sentence as decisive of a theological controversy. But it is not a formal treatise, but a sacred literature; and so it is not by quoting texts but by saturating our minds with its spirit that we can really use it aright. And if this principle is once recognized, it must necessarily greatly modify our theological methods. We can hardly find a better example of the literal method than Bishop Pearson's book on the Creed. In this well-known work, which has been regarded almost as one of the authoritative standards of the Church of England, which was till lately a text-book for candidates for Holy Orders probably in every diocese in England, and which has been held in high esteem and frequently referred to among Nonconformists, we find the several articles of the Creed first discussed as to their meaning, and then proved by an array of texts, quoted from the Old and New Testament, from poetical and prose writings indiscriminately, and with little reference to the context, very much in the same way as propositions of Euclid might be quoted to establish the articles of a geometrical creed. It would be presumptuous to disparage the learning or the utility of so great and approved a work; but we can hardly doubt that with the decline of literalism its authority must diminish, and that the apologetic literature of the future must be on a somewhat different plan.

Another exegetical labour the value of which is likely to be less highly rated as the more spiritual view of Scripture prevails is that of harmonizing the Gospel narratives. As long as it was held that the Gospels must be construed like a legal document, it was of the highest importance to show that, notwithstanding any apparent discrepancies, the four Evangelical narratives were in absolute and unbroken accord and harmony with each other. And this was accomplished by taking the books to pieces, and fitting the fragments into one another like a child's puzzle, so as to produce a fifth narrative, a compound of the original four, out of which all the life and naturalness had been crushed by vio-

lence. Far be it from me to say that it is not possible
to construct a consistent narrative of the life of Christ
from a rational comparison of the four Gospels on historical principles ; but to force them into a mechanical
agreement by an arbitrary process of re-adjustment is
in fact to destroy both the letter and the spirit. Some
questions, such as the chronology of the Crucifixion in
relation to the Passover, must probably remain always
unsettled ; in some points, it must be admitted that
different Evangelists have followed different versions of
the current Christian tradition : the inscription on the
Cross can be harmonized only by the hypothesis that
not one of the Evangelists has recorded it in its fulness.
But would our faith in Christ stand more firm if the
documents from which we derive our knowledge of His
life and teaching fitted into each other with mechanical
accuracy, so that no question could by possibility arise
as to whether on a particular occasion He healed one
or two blind men, or whether it was as He went into
or as He came out of the city ? [1] If so, must we not
confess that we are thinking more of the letter than of
the spirit, more of the dead record than of the living
power of His gracious words and works ?

Indeed, we are sometimes inclined to put forward
for the Scriptures claims far higher and more exacting
than they make for themselves. If, for example, we

[1] Matt. xx. 30; Mark x. 46 ; Luke xviii. 35 : cf. Renan, " Les
Evangiles," p. 179. Harmonists have sought to escape the difficulty by the hypothesis that Christ healed one blind man as he
entered the city (so Luke), another as He quitted it (so Mark),
and that St. Matthew combined the two events.

look at the use which is made of the Old Testament by
the writers of the New, we shall notice some remarkable
and instructive phenomena. We have seen that both
our Lord and the writers of the New Testament accorded
to the writings of the Old Testament the same authority
and reverence that were generally conceded to them by
the Jews of that time ; and from this point of view it
is important to observe their method of quoting and
referring to them. Our Lord Himself does not appear
to have referred to the Old Testament prophecies with
regard to their fulfilment in detail, but simply as con-
firming His own Messianic claims or as furnishing a
standard of morality with which to compare His own
teaching. But the Evangelists and St. Paul and the
author of the Epistle to the Hebrews make a far wider
use of the writings of the Old Covenant. And with
regard to these quotations two points seem specially
noticeable. In the first place, in the great majority of
cases they are made not from the original Hebrew but
from the Septuagint translation ; where the one differs
from the other they usually follow the translation ; and
in some cases they quote words from the Septuagint to
which there is nothing corresponding in the existing
Hebrew text. By some writers this difficulty has been
so strongly felt that they have maintained that the New
Testament use of the Septuagint confers on it a dignity
which it would otherwise have lacked, and raises it, at
least so far as regards the passages quoted, to the same
level of inspired authority with the Hebrew original.
Few, probably, would be found to adopt this theory

now ; the more reasonable conclusion is this, that the
writers of the New Testament did not regard the Hebrew
text as possessing any special or exclusive sanctity, but
were content to use a version which was sufficient for
literary purposes, but which modern theologians would
certainly not regard as affording an adequate basis for
argument.   But beyond this, there is a yet more striking
phenomenon to be noticed.   The New Testament writers,
and in particular St. Paul, quote the words of the Old
Testament in a sense quite independent of the original
connexion, so that it has even been said of the quotations
in St. Paul's Epistles, that " in no passage is there any
certain evidence that the first connexion was present to
the Apostle's mind." [1]   For example, in 1 Cor. xiv.
St. Paul is speaking of the remarkable manifestation
which had appeared in the Church of Corinth, the
speaking with a tongue, by which persons under strong
spiritual excitement uttered in the congregation sounds
which, whether or not they were words of a foreign
language, were at any rate unintelligible to the hearers ;
and he quotes and applies to this phenomenon the words
of Isaiah, which in the revised version read, " By men of
strange lips [or, in the margin, " with stammering lips "]
and with another tongue will He speak unto this people ;
to whom He said, This is the rest, give ye rest to him
that is weary : and this is the refreshing ; yet they
would not hear."   It is incontestable that the Prophet in
this passage threatens the people that, as they despised
and derided his teaching as being childishly simple—

---

[1] Jowett, " Epistles to Thessalonians, etc.," i. p. 357.

"It is precept upon precept, precept upon precept ; line
upon line, line upon line ; here a little, there a little"—
God will adopt a different method with them, and will
speak to them in quite another language, bringing upon
them the Assyrians, men of strange lips : and he adds
that, though God had offered them rest and refreshing,
yet they would not hear.   This passage, of which the
general meaning in the original is undoubted, St. Paul
adapts to his own purpose, and applies to the Corinthians speaking with a tongue ; and the concluding
words, " Yet they would not hear," which in Isaiah refer
to God's offer of rest, St. Paul, by omitting a clause, connects with the tongues.   " In the Law it is written, By
men of strange tongues and by the lips of strangers will
I speak unto this people ; and not even thus will they
hear me, saith the Lord.   Wherefore tongues are for a
sign, not to them that believe, but to the unbelieving."
Here the connexion is evidently purely verbal : there
is no kind of spiritual analogy between the threatened
invasion of Judah by men of foreign tongue and the
utterance in the Corinthian Church of speech unintelligible to the people.   Are we to suppose that the
Prophet Isaiah, when threatening the Jewish people
with punishment for the contempt of the Divine message,
was supernaturally guided to use words which should be
applicable in a quite different sense to a quite different
set of circumstances ?   Surely not.   But then the only
alternative to this hypothesis is that St. Paul made what
we may call a purely literary use of the Old Testament,
not scrupling to avail himself of it without any reference

to its original meaning. Or take St. Paul's quotation
from Genesis [1] in Rom. iv.: "Abraham believed God, and
it was reckoned to him [or, as it is in the original,
"He counted it to him"] for righteousness." St. Paul's
argument is, that Abraham was justified before God, not
by works, but by faith ; and he refers to the passage in
which God promises him an heir, and descendants as
many as the stars; "and he believed in the Lord; and
He counted it to him for righteousness." Here the connexion is much more than verbal ; but, at the same time,
it does not appear that the original necessarily means
more than this—that Abraham believed God's promise,
and God was pleased with him. But this statement St.
Paul enlarges, and adopts as the basis of a theological
argument that Abraham was justified by faith, and,
further, that as he had not yet received circumcision
when righteousness was thus reckoned to him, he was
the father of them that believe, though they be not
circumcised. Or once more, in the veil which Moses
put over his face to mitigate the brightness with which
it shone when he came down from the mount, St. Paul
sees the veil which is upon the heart of Israel, and
which hinders them from seeing the glory of Christ
when Moses is read. [2] In all these, and in many other
instances which might be referred to, St. Paul uses the
utmost freedom in his treatment of the Old Testament.
It is true that this freedom is quite in accordance with
the use of writers of his age, to whom the meaning
of an ancient text was somewhat indeterminate, and

[1] Gen. xv. 6. [2] 2 Cor. iii. 13.

capable of being modified according to the reader's point of view; but none the less it is difficult to reconcile with any modern system of Scripture exegesis, and it points to the conclusion that St. Paul regarded the Old Testament not as a living organism, but as an ancient geological formation, out of which he was at liberty to cut the fragments which suited him, and to arrange them in a fresh setting, in which new colours were reflected from them by the light of the Gospel of the glory of Christ.

And in this lies the defence of what to us may seem fanciful and illogical in St. Paul's method. He took little account of the literal sense, the letter of the Old Testament, because to him the books spoke only of Christ and His Church. To him Christ was all, and in all; the details were of small importance. And though to us, with our more severely logical methods, it is impossible thus to ignore the letter, yet in interpreting St. Paul himself we may at least bear in mind that with his eager impetuous nature we ought not to look for carefully balanced and elaborated statements of doctrine: that his whole mind was possessed with the central idea of Christ, and that to this all else was subordinate; and that therefore his object is rather to set forth the glory of God in Christ Jesus than to explain difficulties or to define mysteries. We may perhaps find an illustration of this in his treatment of the doctrine of predestination in the Epistle to the Romans (ix.–xi.). In writing of the love of God in Christ Jesus, the thought suddenly flashed upon him, ' But what of those, God's elder

people, my kinsmen after the flesh? How can I thus
exalt the glories of the New Covenant without being
disloyal to my own nation?' In feeling after an escape
from this difficulty, he thinks first of the origin of the
Hebrew nation, how from the beginning there had been
a process of selection—how Isaac had been chosen and
not Ishmael, how Jacob the younger had been chosen
instead of Esau the elder son; and from this he infers
that we are not to question the righteousness of God's
choice, "that it is not of him that willeth, nor of
him that runneth, but of God that hath mercy." And
in the end he comes round to the great conclusion that
God's mercy is over all His works; that He has concluded all, Jews and Gentiles alike, in unbelief, that He
may have mercy upon all. But on his way to this conclusion he has given utterance to expressions which, if
regarded not as *obiter dicta* but as fundamental principles, may easily be made the basis of a system fatal
to all effective belief in God's love and righteousness—
"He hath mercy on whom He will, and whom He will
He hardeneth." "What if God, willing to shew His
wrath, and to make His power known, endured with
much long-suffering vessels of wrath fitted unto destruction?" These and like phrases, taken by themselves
and exalted into theological dogmas, have agitated the
Christian Church for centuries with barren controversies,
and filled men's minds with dark thoughts of God.
How large a space this subject filled in the mind of the
sixteenth and seventeenth centuries is indicated by the
fact that the longest and most laboured of the Thirty-

nine Articles is that on Predestination and Election, and that in an exposition of the Apostles' Creed published in 1603, and held in high repute at that time, the Article of the Holy Catholic Church resolves itself into a very full and and minute discussion of predestination and reprobation.[1] The controversy has yielded to the onward movement of Christian thought, and to a worthier view of God's eternal purpose in Christ Jesus ; and men have come to see that in St. Paul's words, read not after the letter but after the spirit, there lies no such doctrine of terror as was found in them by the stern theology of Augustine and of Calvin, but rather an assertion of the power and of the righteousness and of the love of God.

In this case it is most true that " the letter killeth." The terrible doctrine that, " By the decree of God, for the manifestation of His glory, some men are pre-destinated unto everlasting life, and others foreordained to everlasting death,"[2] has done more than anything else to distort men's idea of the Fatherly love of God, and to kill that "joy in the Holy Spirit" which is so essential an element in the Kingdom of God : and yet even here we may acknowledge that the dispensation of the letter had its place in the economy of God's provi-dence. There are times, and both the fourth and the sixteenth centuries were such times, when the minds of men need to be braced by the assertion of God's

[1] Perkins, " A Golden Chaine : containing the Order of the Causes of Salvation and Damnation."
[2] " Westminster Confession."

sovereignty, when force can be secured only by somewhat of narrowness and compression : and such a character as that of Cromwell in history, or of David Deans
in fiction,—hard, stern, inflexible, intolerant of all un-
righteousness,—though not the highest type of human
goodness, is yet, like the Law itself, a needful preparation
for the righteousness of Christ.   Yet here, also, " the
Spirit giveth life."   The belief in God's absolute
sovereignty, when combined with a belief in His perfect
righteousness and love, has the same kind of effect upon
the moral character that an entire confidence in their
commander has upon soldiers.   It gives steadfastness of
purpose, contempt of obstacles, clearness of moral judgment, persistency of effort, indomitable and enthusiastic
hope.   Perhaps some more spiritual form of a belief in
predestination may prove to be the moral tonic for lack
of which there is now so much half-heartedness, so much
coldness of faith.

In this, as in many other points, the teaching of
St. Paul has suffered through being looked at in the
light of later controversy.   His phrases have become
watchwords of religious factions, and we need to go
back to his own day and to listen to his Epistles as they
were first read fresh from the Apostle's heart in the little
gatherings of the faithful at Corinth or Rome, and to
forget all the later accretions of theological association
which have gathered round them.   What, for example,
did St. Paul mean by justification by faith apart from
the deeds of the Law ?   Why was the revival, the re-
discovery of this doctrine in the sixteenth century able

F

to shake the Papal power through half Europe, and why does it now sound archaic, technical, unreal ? Is it not because we associate the words with burnt-out controversies, and forget to ask whether they do not contain a principle which is as fresh and living for us as for the first or the sixteenth century ? If St. Paul was writing merely against Jewish observances in his own day, or, by anticipation, against the formal penances or the pilgrimages or the indulgences of the mediæval Church, then, indeed, the words have little meaning for us ; but, if he meant by justification by faith, that man looks on the outward appearance, but God looks on the heart ; if he meant that God appraises the moral value of men's acts by the inner spring and motive, and that He judges men, not by what they profess, nor by what they seem, but by what they are, then surely " that we are justified by faith only is a most wholesome doctrine and very full of comfort," and may still be regarded as the test of a standing or a falling Church.

There is another doctrine of the New Testament in which the distinction between the letter and the spirit is very marked and very important,—I mean the doctrine of the second coming of Christ. In the great discourse spoken by our Lord on the Mount of Olives over against the Temple, which is recorded in various proportions by the three synoptic Evangelists, while it is clear that the foreground sets before us the approaching destruction of the holy city, there also looms in the background the faint foreshadowing of another event, the coming of the Son of Man. How far our Lord meant by that simply the final dissolution of the Jewish polity and the dispersion of the nation—and that He had this in His mind we may infer from His words, "This generation shall not pass away till all things be accomplished,"—and how far He meant also to point to a great final coming—

> " To that far-off Divine event
> To which the whole creation moves,"

is a question which need not be discussed now. Clearly His words to Pilate, " Henceforth ye shall see the Son of man sitting at the right hand of power, and coming in the clouds of heaven," point not to a far-off and momentary vision, but to the sight and acknowledgment of His power in the foundation of His kingdom. But however this may be, we cannot fail to see that there was in the Church from the beginning an expectation that the generation then living would see with their bodily eyes Christ coming in the clouds, and would hear with their bodily ears the voice of the Archangel and the trumpet of God. It was, indeed, a very natural belief; for to them the spiritual world was the only reality, the things which were not seen were alone eternal, the things which were seen must soon pass away. And though the experience of eighteen centuries has taught us that in this the first Christians were misled by the very vividness of their faith, yet there still clings to the belief of the Church something of the gross and material element in respect of the coming of Christ. But if in respect of the When the Church has been led to modify its expectation, is it not reasonable also to suppose that in regard to the How a like modification must take place ? Not to dwell upon the argument that the change in our conception of the earth and the heavens must involve a corresponding modification of all physical and local ideas and relations, we may surely accept the majestic simplicity of the words of the *Te Deum*, " We believe that Thou shalt come to be our Judge," without encumbering our belief with any literalisms such as the artists of the Middle Ages delighted to portray. It is, indeed, worth noticing to how great an extent Christian eschatology has been moulded by the outward circumstances and by the culture and intelligence of the age. In days of oppression and persecution men have drawn comfort and hope from the thought that Christ's coming could not be long delayed, and have cried, " Lord Jesus, come quickly," and have looked eagerly for the sign of the Son of Man in heaven. In days when theology was systematized and the kingdom of Heaven assumed the form of a feudal monarchy,[1] men imagined a magnified and glorified court of justice, in which apostles, martyrs, confessors, monks, and virgins should sit as assessors or more than assessors with the Judge, and should take part in the judgment

---

[1] Cf. Thomas Aquinas, " Elucid.," c. 70: " Qualiter veniet Dominus ad judicium? Sicut Imperator ingressurus civitatem, corona ejus et alia insignia praeferuntur, per quae adventus ejus cognoscitur; ita Christus in ea forma, qua ascendit, cum Ordinibus omnibus Angelorum ad judicium veniens. Angeli crucem ejus ferentes praeibunt, mortuos tuba et voce in occursum ejus excitabunt." Cf. also Milman, " Latin Christianity," vi., p. 227, sqq.

of the nations who should be gathered at the judgment seat.   In days of rude literalism, the terrors of judgment were enhanced by the resources of sculpture and painting, and hideous demons fanned the fire and fed the furnace for the fiercer torturing of lost souls.   It may be that in our days of laxity of moral fibre, when good does not appear so indisputably good, nor evil so absolutely evil, there is a tendency to put aside the thought of judgment to come, and to regard all looking forward as unprofitable speculation, and to concentrate all our thoughts upon this present world.   We do not know, indeed, and it would not be useful to inquire, how much of the words of St. Paul and of our Lord on this subject is parabolic and how much literal; it is enough to believe that there will be a revelation of the righteous judgment of God, who will render to every man according to his deeds.

"The letter killeth, but the spirit giveth life."   We cannot, indeed, doubt that even as the blind veneration of the Church was an instrument in God's hands for training men to something better and purer, so the blind veneration of the Bible, which has prevailed since the Reformation, has been a valuable factor in the formation of the Christian character.   The term "Bible Christians," though it has been degraded to serve as the name of an obscure sect, is no unfair description of a very high and noble type of Christian people, of whom in our own country we may name as examples, Wesley, and Wilberforce, and Simeon, and Cecil, and Scott, and Newton.   To these men, the word of God as contained

in the Scriptures was the very pivot upon which their
life turned.   In it they sought, and sought not in vain,
the motive power by which to raise their generation to
a higher level.   They knew the Bible thoroughly ; they
accepted its authority absolutely and unquestioningly ;
they taught it unceasingly ; they tried themselves by
its standard ; they lived by its precepts.   And it is
certain that they did a great and lasting work.   Other
influences, no doubt, have been at work ; but no one
who knows anything of the history of the eighteenth
and nineteenth centuries will deny that to the Evangelical revival was due the beginning of that upward
movement which we trust is far from having reached its
highest point.   But though the work of these men lasts,
though we look back to them as noble examples of
Christian holiness, yet not only is the special form of
religious life which they illustrate no longer largely
influential, but where it exists it tends to be obstructive,
unprogressive, unfruitful.   And if we ask why this is
so, why a phase of religious energy which once seemed
able to move the world has lost its power, is not the
answer this, that they practically held that when the
last word of the last book of the Canon of the New
Testament was written, God ceased to reveal Himself to
man ; that they were so engrossed with the letter that
they failed to see that the Spirit of God is still leading
men into all the truth, that He has never ceased to
teach the Church by the experience of history, by the
light of science, by the widening of men's thoughts with
the progress of the suns, by the new knowledge and the

new forms of industry and of social life which His creative power opens up ?

For this surely is the essential distinction which separates Christianity from all other religions and reve- lations—that whereas they profess to be complete and final, the Christian revelation consists not in a book, but in a life and a spirit; it is "incomprehensible," not to be adequately and completely measured and ex- pressed in any form of words, not to be limited by the conceptions of any age or Church.   Though heaven and earth pass away, Christ's words shall not pass away, because they are spirit and they are life.

This would appear to be the true reply to those who would place Mohammedanism in any kind of competi- tion or rivalry with Christianity.   It is not to be denied that in many respects the religion of Islam teaches a very high and pure morality ; that it has laid hold on races which Christianity has not been able to touch ; that it " wrought a great religious and social reforma- tion among the pagan Arabs ; " that its effect on its modern converts is a salutary one.   But it is a religion of the letter and not of the spirit ; it has not in it the capacity of development, of self-adaptation ; it has no fitness to become a universal religion.   In its best days it has produced a brilliant civilization ; it has fostered science and literature ; there have been times when it seemed as though Islam were more progressive than Christianity : but it has upon it the mark of finality ; it is not, it can never become, the religion of humanity ; and it lacks the one supreme sanction, the great motive

force which Christ attached to His law—" If ye love Me,
keep My commandments."

> " Mohammed's truth lay in a holy Book,
>   Christ's in a sacred life.
> So while the world rolls on from change to change,
>   And realms of thought expand,
> The letter stands without expanse or range,
>   Stiff as a dead man's hand;
> While, as the life-blood fills the growing form,
>   The Spirit Christ has shed
> Flows through the ripening ages fresh and warm,
>   More felt than heard or read.
> And therefore, though ancestral sympathies
>   And closest ties of race
> May guard Mohammed's precepts and decrees
>   Through many a tract of space,
> Yet in the end the tight-drawn line must break,
>   The sapless tree must fall,
> Nor let the form one time did well to take
>   Be tyrant over all." [1]

Probably the best hope that we can form for the
exegesis of the future is that it should be literal in the
sense of understanding the text of Scripture according
to the ordinary rules of interpretation applied to other
writings, and spiritual in the sense of seeking to extract
from the local and temporary and personal accidents the
eternal principles of truth which these contain.   In the
Old Testament it will perhaps be less occupied in point-
ing out how this or that detail in the Mosaic ritual
referred to Christ, or how this or that prophecy was
fulfilled in His life, and more in showing how God, for
the sake of all nations, trained and educated Israel by

[1] Lord Houghton's " Poems."

the object-lessons of worship and sacrifice, by the poetry
of the Psalmists, by the lofty moral teaching of the
Prophets, to receive and to transmit to the world His
great revelation of Himself in Jesus Christ. It will
approach the New Testament without *à priori* theories
of inspiration, and will endeavour from a consideration
of the actual phenomena of the books to ascertain their
place in the economy of the spiritual kingdom. It will
recognize in the Bible very various degrees of spiritual
enlightenment; it will not, like the Puritans, find
maxims of modern politics in the Hebrew Prophets, nor
the minutiæ of Christian theology in the Hebrew
Psalmists; it will not mistake poetry for prose, nor the
voices of men for the Voice of God; above all, if it is to
be fruitful, it will seek to be led by the Living Spirit
into all truth, and will acknowledge with St. Augustine,
that he will best understand Scripture whose heart is
full of love.[1]

There seems reason to fear that the habitual study of
Scripture as a necessity of the spiritual life is more rare
than it was formerly. If so, it is a thing much to be
lamented. If we have laid aside some superstitious and
mechanical theories of inspiration, if we have learnt that
the Word of God comes to us not only in the Bible, but
also in the inward voice of the Spirit and in the discipline
of His providence throughout our lives, yet we have not
outgrown, we can never outgrow, the teaching of Christ

---

[1] Aug., Serm. ccl.: "Divinarum scripturarum multiplicem
abundantiam, latissimamque doctrinam, sine ullo errore compre-
hendit, et sine ullo labore custodit, cujus cor plenum est caritate."

and of His Apostles.   If in the past the Bible has been
misunderstood through bondage to the letter, that should
encourage us to study it more earnestly under the
freedom of the spirit.   To quote the words of Bishop
Temple, "the immediate work of our day is the study
of the Bible.   Other studies will act upon the progress
of mankind by acting through and upon this.   For while
a few highly educated men here and there, who have
given their minds to special pursuits, may think the
study of the Bible a thing of the past, yet assuredly, if
their science is to have its effect upon men in the mass,
it must be by affecting their moral and religious convic-
tions.   In no other way have men been, or can men be,
deeply and permanently changed.   But though this
study must be for the present and for some time the
centre of all studies, there is meanwhile no study of
whatever kind which will not have its share in the
general effect." [1]   Since those words were written, nearly
thirty years ago, all other studies in the University have
received a notable impulse.   Let it not be said that the
study of Scripture languishes.   In the new world which
is coming upon us, the world in which the younger
among us will have to take their part, it will be more
than ever needful that the scribe who hath been made
a disciple unto the kingdom of Heaven should bring
forth out of his treasure things new and old: the new
science of religion, of language, of textual criticism, of
the laws of nature ; and the old reverence, the old
godliness, the old familiarity with the text of Scripture.

[1] " Essays and Reviews," p. 48.

In the two great uprisings of the English people, the
ecclesiastical revolt of the sixteenth and the political of
the seventeenth century, the letter of the Bible exercised
a vast influence.   God grant that in the great social
movements which this and the coming age are likely to
witness, the spirit of the Bible may act not less power-
fully upon the minds and actions of men.

LECTURE IV.

IN THE CHURCH.

"For he is not a Jew, which is one outwardly; neither is that circumcision, which is outward in the flesh : but he is a Jew, which is one inwardly; and circumcision is that of the heart, in the spirit, and not in the letter: whose praise is not of men, but of God."— Rom. ii. 28.

BEFORE entering upon our subject to-day, it will be well to recall as briefly as possible the main points of the previous lectures.

From a consideration of the passages in which St. Paul uses the terms "letter" and "spirit," we saw that primarily he means by the letter the fixed, rigid, unchangeable code which was the basis of the Jewish polity, the system which he commonly sums up under the name of the Law, under which he had himself been brought up, and which, since he had been delivered from it, he had come to regard with something like personal animosity, as a grown man might regard a harsh tutor who, with the best of motives, had oppressed him and made him miserable in his boyhood. And by the spirit we saw that he meant that Living Force which is the ever-present inspiration of the Christian life, not the

law of a carnal commandment, but the power of an endless life.[1]   But from this root-idea we traced the growth
of the later use of the terms, to denote the distinction
between that which is fixed, unchangeable, and therefore
transitory, and that which has the capacity of growth
and development and therefore of permanence, in enact-
ments, institutions, customs, polities.   We recognized
the same two elements under varying forms in Church
history, in human life and thought, and in the changed
and changing life of this University.   And passing on,
in the second and third lectures, to the letter and the
spirit in Scripture exegesis, we discussed the Jewish
view of the Sacred Books of the Old Covenant, and its
influence on the Christian Church ; and having spoken
of the allegorical method of interpretation, and its
tendency to sacrifice the letter to the supposed spiritual
sense, I indicated what appears to be the true view of
Scripture, that it is not a formal theological treatise but
a sacred literature ; and I showed from several instances
how we should apply the principle of the supremacy of
the spirit over the letter to the interpretation of the
New Testament writings.   To-day I propose to consider
the contrast between the letter and the spirit, between
the unchangeable and formal and the variable and
spiritual element, in reference to the kingdom of Christ.

The distinction between the end and the means is
one which is very familiar to us in theory, but which
practically is very liable to be overlooked.   As objects
nearer to the eye seem larger than those more remote, so

[1] Heb. vii. 16.

there is a tendency for the means to shut out the view
of the end, and to become ends in themselves. This is
conspicuously the case in political matters. Persons
associate together for the sake of some object or for
the promotion of some political principle, but soon the
association itself takes the place of the object, and it
is thought more necessary to support the party than to
promote the ends for which the party came into existence. And in the same way laws and observances
survive the purpose for which they were created, and are
kept up when that purpose is either attained or forgotten.
And perhaps this tendency is still stronger in the case
of institutions and observances connected with religion,
because these are naturally apt to become invested with
a sacred character, and to have ascribed to them a value
and an importance independent of their object. The
whole history of religion is full of instances of the way
in which things originally designed simply as means to
an end become ends in themselves and the original end
is lost sight of. The Sabbath, designed as a beneficent
interval of rest for the servants, the cattle, and the
stranger, has become to the modern Jew a burdensome
and meaningless formality. Prayer, the communion of
the human with the Divine Spirit, has often degenerated
into the mere saying of offices, the telling of beads, the
unintelligent repetition of Paternosters and Aves, or the
turning of a wheel on which prayers are inscribed.
"Omnia fatis in pejus ruere;" there is a downward
tendency in things, which, unless counteracted by the
living power of the Spirit, will drag down the highest

and holiest things till they become meaningless and
useless. And therefore in respect of all institutions,
organizations, observances, whether religious, social,
political, or of whatever kind, it is necessary to ask
what is their original meaning and purpose ? For what
were they founded ? Have they in any way swerved
from their original intention, and if so, has it been a
legitimate deflection or not ? What in them is essential
and what accidental ? What is part of the original
institution, and what is the after-growth and accretion
of later times ? For there is no such thing as a Divine
right for any institution whatever to exist independently
of the object for which it exists. If it fails through any
inherent incapacity to fulfil that object, it is condemned ;
if it fails partially from causes which are removable, it
requires reform ; if other institutions fulfil it equally
well, they have established a *prima-facie* right to exist
side by side with it.

We must not suppose that the most venerable of
institutions, the Church of Christ, is exempt from such
inquiry as to its object and its methods : for the Church,
though Divine in its origin and its consummation, is still
a human society, and all that is human is liable to decay
and renewal and change and growth. The legitimacy
of this inquiry is admitted by Cardinal Newman himself, when he argues that it is impossible to conceive of
ultra-Protestantism as developed out of primitive Christianity. It is possible, indeed, in the political sphere to
evade its force by arguing that an institution which has
outlived its original purpose may yet be preserved for

the sake of some collateral advantage, or some new function to which it has adapted itself: hereditary monarchy, for example, if it is no longer useful for giving to government the vigour and unity of purpose which comes of its being centred in a single hand, may well be defended on the ground that it connects us with the past, that it is an impressive symbol of the unity of the commonwealth, or that it saves us from the mischievous intrigues that might result from an elective headship of the State; but in the case of religious institutions no deflection from first principles is permissible, if we believe that those first principles are of Divine authority and rest on an eternal basis.

Strictly speaking, we as Christians possess one and one only religious institution—the Church. All else, the the Faith, the Scriptures, the Sacraments, the Ministry, the ordinances of worship, the beneficent organizations, are but departments and functions of the one Catholic Church. And it therefore becomes a question of primary importance, What is the true end and object, what is the essence, of the Christian Church?

We shall probably not be far from the mark if we say that the end for which the Church exists is the perfecting of redeemed humanity. To this all is subordinate; whatever does not directly or indirectly conduce to this is no essential function of the Church; whatever makes for this end ought to be claimed as part of the Church's work. It will not be necessary now to enlarge upon this point, but it is well that it should be clearly stated and borne in mind, that it may guide us

in discussing the further question, What is essential and
what is accidental in the framework and constitution of
the Church ?

It has been lately said by an eminent representative
of Nonconformity,[1] whose presence in Oxford is a
welcome sign of the times, that "there is no evidence
that Jesus ever created, or thought of creating, an
organized society. There is no idea he so little empha-
sizes as the idea of the Church. He uses the term but
twice—once in the local or congregational sense, and
once in the universal, but only so as to define His own
sole authority and supremacy. His familiar idea is the
kingdom of God or of Heaven ; but this kingdom is
without organization, and incapable of being organized.
. . . It is essentially the contrary and contrast of what
is now understood as the Church, whether Catholic or
Anglican." It is certain that Dr. Fairbairn does not
reject the idea of religious organization : what he means
apparently is, that Christ Himself did not found or even
contemplate an organized society. That He did not
found one will be admitted by all ; that He did not
contemplate one is difficult to suppose, in view of his
words, "On this rock I will build My Church." For
οἰκοδομεῖν ἐκκλησίαν are hardly words that could be
used of the mere implanting in the world of a new
principle of spiritual life ; and if we accept the mission
of the Holy Spirit as a part of Christ's work, and if,
further, we admit that the Christian people were to be
builded together for an habitation of God in the Spirit,

---

[1] Dr. Fairbairn, in *Contemporary Review*, July, 1885.

then it would seem to follow that the formation of a
society was contemplated by Christ ; and a society
without organization is something like a contradiction
in terms.   Indeed, the new commandment which Christ
gave to His disciples—" That ye love one another ; as
I have loved you, that ye also love one another " —involves the establishment of very close relations between
His disciples.   The very first words of His prayer, " Our
Father," imply that those who use it are joined together
as members of a family.   And though in a family there
is no formal organization, and all authority proceeds
directly from the father, yet there is a kind of informal
and spontaneous division of offices which answers very
much to what appears to have been the gradual process
of development of offices in the Church.

And this seems to point to the true theory of the
constitution of the Christian Church.   It is at once a
family and a kingdom : a family, because from the one
Father all fatherhood and brotherhood, all human
relations, are derived ; a kingdom, because all authority
is derived from the King, all government centres in
Him.   And just as in the English monarchy the existing
forms of government were evolved gradually and, as it
were, spontaneously, in accordance with the requirements
of the national life, so that what we call the constitution
is no formally contrived system, but the outgrowth of
circumstances : so the constitution of the Christian
Church is not a Divinely appointed order in the sense of
having been imposed by a command of Christ, or by an
ordinance of the Apostles, but rather the result of the

conditions of the Christian society ; it is a form of polity which we can, not without difficulty, but yet with reasonable probability, trace the origin and development, an organization which in any stage of its history involves the possibility of further development, of progressive adaptation to the changing circumstances of the Church, an institution, not of the letter, not fixed and stereotyped for all time, but of the spirit, capable of assuming new shapes without any breach of historic continuity.

The question whether a given form of organization is of the essence of the Church of Christ, so that we can sharply define the Church as that body of Christian people which possesses a threefold ministry with direct organic succession from the Apostles, to which the Roman Church would add the further qualification of submission to the see of Rome ; or whether the Church in its essence is simply the association of those who profess belief in Christ and obedience to Him, organization being, indeed, in the nature of things indispensable, and yet an accident not bound up in the nature of the institution, is one which lies at the root of our conception of Christianity. For it makes the whole difference to that conception whether we hold, on the one hand, that Christ did, either directly or through His Apostles, institute a form of government by which His Church was to be characterized and distinguished until His coming again, or, on the other hand, that He put into men's hearts and wrote on their minds a law—the law of love—which should draw them together in one body, and left them free to organize themselves under the

formative guiding and influence of the Spirit. It is a
question on which practical issues depend. If the former
theory be the true one, the Christian Church at the
present day is confined to the Greek, the Roman, and
the Anglican communions, and a vast proportion of the
most intelligent and active-minded Christians in the
United States, in the Colonies, and on the Continent
of Europe are outside the Church's pale. If, on the
contrary, we accept the latter theory, it must be
admitted that from a very early period in the history
of Christianity the letter began to prevail over the
spirit, and that for many centuries the true idea of the
kingdom of Heaven was obscured by the growth of a
vast organization, admirably adapted for the age from
which it sprang, and being undoubtedly a part of God's
providential order, yet being after all only a phase, a
temporary and partial presentment of that kingdom of
Heaven which it claimed to embody completely and
exclusively. Which of these difficulties is the greater
may be discussed later; but at least it may be said,
that on those who accept the Reformation there lies no
obligation to represent the Church as having attained
to a full comprehension of the truth otherwise than
gradually and painfully, or as having been free from
much superstition and many unworthy conceptions of
God and of His kingdom.

I propose to consider first the historical argument,
and then the general spirit and tone of the New Testament.

It is undoubtedly true that, so far as the existing

documents can be trusted as adequate records, Christ
Himself gave no directions whatever as to matters of
Church organization. It has indeed been argued that
this must have been among the things pertaining to
the kingdom of God, of which our Lord spoke to His
disciples after His resurrection. But to this it may be
replied, that this is an unsupported assumption, and
that when He does speak of the kingdom of God or of
Heaven, it is without any reference whatever to any
material framework or organization. So that for the
intention of Christ and His Apostles we are thrown
back upon the general spirit and tendency of their teaching and practice, as recorded in the Gospels, the
Epistles, and the Acts of the Apostles. And in order
to form to ourselves an idea of this spirit and tendency,
we must endeavour to put out of sight for a moment all
the accretions of eighteen centuries of Church history,
and to place ourselves in the position of those who saw
the works and heard the words of Christ, or of those
who in the little assemblies of Christian believers
listened to the letters written by " Paul, an Apostle not
from men, neither through man, but through Jesus
Christ, and God the Father," and so to gather, as it were
at first hand, what was in their thoughts when they
spoke or wrote of the kingdom of Heaven.

Jesus came into Galilee, preaching the Gospel of the
kingdom of God, and saying, "The time is fulfilled, and
the kingdom of God is at hand ; repent ye, and believe
the Gospel." And when He has gathered round Him a
little band of followers, He sends them forth to preach

that the kingdom of Heaven is at hand. Of that kingdom He gave no definition, but many descriptions.
The parables of the tares, the mustard seed, the leaven,
the hidden treasure, the pearl, the draw-net; of the
labourers in the vineyard, of the wicked husbandmen,
of the marriage of the king's son, and of the ten virgins,
are expressly introduced by Him as likenesses of the
kingdom of Heaven. The idea of a kingdom was no
doubt borrowed from the Old Covenant, in which Israel
was sharply marked off as God's special people and
kingdom, in contrast to the nations round about; and
so the kingdom of Heaven in the New Covenant would
mean that order of things in which God's will should
be the law, and His purpose of redemption should be
carried out. On the other hand, it is remarkable that
when the disciples use the term, they at once import
into it the idea of organization and personal preferment.
"The disciples came to Jesus, saying, Who is the
greatest in the kingdom of Heaven?"[1] And He pointed
out to them that their state of mind was quite incompatible with being subjects of the kingdom. "Except
ye be converted"—except your whole attitude be
changed—"and ye become as little children, ye shall not
enter into the kingdom of Heaven." A significant indication, surely, of the change which was destined to
come over the conception of the kingdom, as soon as it
passed from the mind of the Master into those of His
disciples! In Christ's mouth, the kingdom of Heaven
is the carrying out of the true relation of mankind to

[1] Matt. xviii. 1.

God ; in the mouth of the disciples, it is the hierarchy
in which, as in earthly kingdoms, those who are nearest
to the King shall enjoy a supremacy over the rest. The
only idea of pre-eminence of which Christ ever speaks is
that of those who had followed Him and continued with
Him in His temptations, who should eat and drink at
His table in His kingdom, and sit on thrones judging
the twelve tribes of Israel. It is, in fact, true in the
strictest sense to say, that the kingdom of Heaven in
our Lord's conception is independent of organization.
He spoke of the kingdom of God, not as a thing which
should hereafter grow up, but as being already in their
midst. He was among them, and "Ubi Christus, ibi
ecclesia." [1] The binding principle of His kingdom was
love to God and love to man : its charter was, "Where
two or three are gathered together in My Name, there
am I in the midst of them." The guarantee of its permanence was His promise that, when His visible Presence was removed, He would send the Paraclete to
abide with His people for ever. And accordingly, after
His departure, we find the disciples united together, not
merely by the animating memory of the past, but by
the living and penetrating and pervading influence of
the Divine Spirit ; the kingdom of God took visible
shape in a society. Of this society the Apostles were
the appointed and natural leaders ; and to their company was soon added one who laboured more abun-

---

[1] Ὅπου ἂν ᾖ Χριστὸς Ἰησοῦς, ἐκεῖ ἡ καθολικὴ ἐκκλησία (Ignat.
ad Smyrn., 8). This seems to be the earliest mention of the
Catholic Church.

dantly than they all, one who was not a whit behind
the chiefest Apostles, Paul of Tarsus, the Apostle of the
Gentiles. By his energy were gathered Churches in the
cities of Asia Minor and of the Mediterranean seaboard ;
and it is in them that we are able to trace, through the
medium of his letters, the growth of the earliest Church
organization.

Let us turn for a moment to the phenomena which
are discernible in them.

In the Epistle to the Philippians, St. Paul sends
greeting to the saints in Christ Jesus with the bishops
and deacons. The same names appear in the Pastoral
Epistles, where also elders or presbyters are spoken of.
And in the Acts of the Apostles St. Paul sends from
Miletus to Ephesus and summons the presbyters of the
Church, whom in addressing them he calls bishops.
And St. Peter, in writing to the presbyters as a fellow-
presbyter, alludes to their office as that of the Episcopate. So far we find three official names in use—
Bishops, Presbyters, Deacons. But it is now universally
conceded that the first two belong to one and the same
office, the argument on behalf of modern Episcopacy
being that the name of Bishop was gradually detached
from the Presbyters, and was applied exclusively to
those chief pastors who succeeded to the Apostles in the
general oversight and government of the Churches. Up
to this point, the matter might seem tolerably simple.
But in two other important Epistles the phenomena
seem to point in a different direction. In the First
Epistle to the Corinthians, St. Paul, in writing of the

work of the Spirit in the Church, says, "God hath set some in the Church, first apostles, secondly prophets, thirdly teachers, then miracles, then gifts of healings, helps, governments, divers kinds of tongues." It is, of course, possible to argue that these were some of them extraordinary and all of them temporary offices, which were afterwards drawn up and remoulded into the permanent organization of the Church ; but it seems difficult to believe that these offices, which, as we cannot but observe, are catalogued with singular precision and formality, "First apostles, secondly prophets, thirdly teachers," co-existed either in the same or in different persons with the other and more permanent offices of presbyters and deacons. In the Epistle which is inscribed to the Ephesians, St. Paul says, "Unto each one of us was the grace given according to the measure of the gift of Christ. . . . And he gave some to be apostles ; and some, prophets ; and some, evangelists ; and some pastors and teachers : for the perfecting of the saints, unto the work of ministering, unto the building up of the body of Christ." Here the offices seem somewhat less difficult to reconcile with those of the presbyterate and diaconate which, according to the First Epistle to Timothy,[1] appear to have existed at Ephesus not much later ; but if we look at the allusions to Church organization in the Acts and the Epistles without

---

[1] It is unnecessary to discuss the genuineness of the First Epistle to Timothy. Even M. Renan, who adopts the conclusions of the Tubingen school against it, frequently quotes it as historical evidence.

any tendency to interpret them into conformity with later history, we must certainly admit that, while ecclesiastical offices seem already to be taking some a purely local and others a more general character, it is difficult to find any sanction to any one form of Church government, and that, in Hooker's words, " In tying the Church to the orders of the Apostles' times, they tie it to a marvellous uncertain rule." [1] The Churches undoubtedly had their several organizations, not apparently the same everywhere ; the Church as yet had none.

After the close of the New Testament Canon, Church history is like one of those streams in certain geological formations, which disappear underground, the course of which can only be conjectured from the direction which they are found to be taking when they emerge again to the light.   We can discern something of the course of things in St. Paul's time ; from the writings of the so-called Apostolic Fathers, and of Tertullian, and from the Teaching of the twelve Apostles, we can perceive that much must have happened in the interval; but there is a break between the Apostolic and the sub-Apostolic age in which we have no documentary evidence to guide us. Without entering on any full discussion of the origin of the Christian ministry—a discussion which, indeed, is somewhat wide of our subject—we may say that by the end of the second decade of the second century we see manifesting itself in the Church at large a tendency to Episcopacy, in the sense of a single ruler in each Church, acting as President of the Council of

[1] Hooker, "Eccl. Pol.," bk. i., c. ii., § 2.

Presbyters; and by the end of the second century we
cannot fail to recognize Episcopal government as characteristic of the Church.   Indeed, it will hardly be
seriously disputed, that, if any one form of Church
organization possesses exclusive Apostolic sanction and
authority, it is the Episcopal form.   The investigations
of Rothe in Germany, and of Bishop Lightfoot and Dr.
Hatch in England, have so far simplified the question,
that the contention of Cartwright in the sixteenth
century—that Presbyterianism is the only lawful form
of Church government—is hardly likely to be repeated.
The issue now is a comparatively simple one—Is Episcopacy of Divine institution and authority, in any other
sense than that in which it may be predicated of every
settled form of government, ecclesiastical and political,
that it is ordained of God ?

The argument that, if a special form of organization
were essential to the Church, Christ would have given
His disciples definite and clear directions concerning it,
though undoubtedly weighty, may yet be pressed too
far.   For it may be replied, "True, Christ did not Himself
give any directions as to the form which His Church
was to assume, but He promised that the Spirit should
guide them into all truth ; and we find as a matter of
fact that it is to the Spirit's agency that all gifts, both
of government and of teaching in the Church, are
referred."   But the contention goes deeper than this.
If the Christian Dispensation is not of the letter but
of the spirit, if it differs from the Old Dispensation
mainly in this, that whereas the old was a system of

restricted sanctities, in which a particular nation, a particular family, particular days and particular places were set apart as holy, in the New all this is reversed, and all nations, all men, all places, and all times are in principle alike holy, then no form of organization can be essential; it can only concern the *bene esse* and not the *esse* of the Church. This is the principle on which Hooker relies in his great argument against the Puritans. They maintained that no form of Church policy was lawful except the Presbyterian. Hooker replied, not that Episcopacy alone was lawful, but that no form was prescribed as essential, and that therefore Episcopacy was lawful.[1] "He which affirmeth speech to be necessary among all men throughout the world, doth not thereby import that all men must necessarily speak one kind of language. Even so the necessity of polity and regiment in all Churches may be held without holding any one certain form to be necessary in them all."[2] By no one has the spiritual nature of the kingdom of Christ been stated with more luminous clearness or more judicial precision than by Bishop Lightfoot. "The kingdom of Christ, not being a kingdom of this world, is not limited by the restrictions which fetter other societies, political or religious. It is in the fullest sense free, comprehensive, universal. . . . It has no sacred days or seasons, no special sanctuaries, because every time and every place alike are holy. Above all, it has no sacerdotal system. It interposes no sacrificial tribe or class between God and

[1] Hooker, bk. vii., c. ii.
[2] Ibid., bk. iii., c. ii., § i.

man, by whose intervention alone God is reconciled and man forgiven. Each individual member holds personal communion with the Divine Head. To Him immediately he is responsible, and from Him directly he obtains pardon and draws strength." And further, while admitting the necessity for convenience' sake, of appointing special times and places for meetings for worship, he adds, " For communicating instruction and for preserving public order, for conducting religious worship and for dispensing social charities, it became necessary to appoint special officers. But the priestly functions and privileges of the Christian people are never regarded as transferred or even delegated to these officers. They are called stewards or messengers of God, servants or ministers of the Church; but the sacerdotal title is never once conferred on them. The only priests under the Gospel, designated as such in the New Testament, are the saints, the members of the Christian brotherhood." [1]

Here we have, set forth by a great master of theology, a clear statement of the true theory of the Christian ministry. It is not a sacerdotal order; the priestly character belongs to the Christian people at large, and cannot be alienated by or taken away from them; [2] it is not a succession through which a Divine influence is handed on by imposition of hands; it is an

---

[1] Bishop Lightfoot, " Essay on the Christian Ministry."

[2] " The most exalted office in the Church, the highest gift of the Spirit, conveyed no sacerdotal right which was not enjoyed by the humblest member of the Christian community." — Bishop Lightfoot, *loc. cit.*

office and administration pertaining to the whole Christian body, but exercised from the necessity of the case by a certain number "called and chosen to this work by men who have public authority given unto them in the congregation, to call and send ministers into the Lord's vineyard." And therefore in our definition of the Church we are not to introduce as a differentia that it possesses this or that form of ministry, any more than in defining an army we should specify that it must have so many grades of officers : officers of some kind it must have, or it will be a mob and not an army ; but there is no reason in the nature of things why different regiments should not have different grades, some more, some less. And so in respect of Church offices, it is not necessary that they "be in all places one, and utterly alike ;" for the definition of the Church is not tied to a special form of ministry, but "the visible Church of Christ is a congregation of faithful men [*cœtus fidelium*], in which the pure Word of God is preached, and the Sacraments be duly ministered, according to Christ's ordinance in all those things that of necessity are requisite to the same."[1]

It is true, as I have already admitted, that the historical argument appears at first sight strong on the other side. From the time of Cyprian to the time of the Reformation, the Episcopate existed everywhere, and was regarded as an essential element in the Church. But Church history did not begin with Cyprian, neither did it end with the Reformation. Bishop Lightfoot's "Essay

[1] Article XIX.

on the Christian Ministry" indicates how gradually,
and not in all places simultaneously, Episcopal government was evolved : and it is plain that at the Reformation, while the Churches which adhered to the Roman
obedience retained the theory that Catholicity depended
on submission to the Roman See, the Reformed Churches
fell back on the primitive theory that the Church is the
congregation of Christians, and assumed the right of
revising for themselves both their organization and
their doctrinal formulas.   And accordingly for now
more than three centuries we see Christendom divided
no longer into the two great communions of the East
and West, but into a multiplicity of differently organized
bodies, all professing and calling themselves Christian,
all claiming to belong to the universal Church, all aiming
at the promotion of the kingdom of Heaven, yet not
bound together by any outward uniformity.   And we
notice further that it is precisely in those periods and
in those countries where there is most enlightenment,
most progress, most religious and political activity, that
there is least uniformity of religious life.   So that the
historical argument seems to break down, and it is no
longer possible to point to the universal acceptance of
one form of Church government as an argument for its
universal obligation.   The truth appears to be that
Episcopacy in the Ecclesiastical sphere occupies a
position analogous to that of Monarchy in the political.
The writers of the seventeenth century who asserted
the Divine right of Bishops asserted no less strongly
the Divine right of Kings.   And both the scriptural

and the historical arguments were as strong for the one as for the other theory. But the English people rejected the arguments of Sherlock and Sir Robert Filmer. They did not indeed abolish monarchy, but by placing William of Orange on the throne they practically asserted the right of the people to choose its own Government. Thus, in the case of monarchy, the logic of facts has proved too strong for *à priori* theories; and no one now refuses to acknowledge the legitimacy of republican government where it is established by the will of the people. But the Divine right of Episcopacy is still maintained in spite of accomplished facts, and loyalty to the Church is made to consist, not in zeal for righteousness and brotherly love, but in the refusal to acknowledge as Christian ministers all who lack the imposition of Episcopal hands. But to those who believe that God reveals His will not once for all but progressively, by the working of His providence on the course of history, it will not seem reasonable to suppose that the development of Christian life in new forms which dates from the sixteenth century has been an infraction of the Divine plan, and that to accomplish that unity for which Christian people hope and pray, it is necessary to go back three hundred years. I remember some two and twenty years ago hearing a preacher in the Duomo of Florence, whose one panacea for the evils that then afflicted the Church and the world was the oft-repeated refrain, "Submit to the Roman Pontiff." That does not sound very reasonable advice in the light of subsequent events: but is it less

reasonable than the attempt to bring about the unity
of the Spirit by a universal submission to the Episcopate,
Anglican or Roman as the case may be? Can we look
at Christendom as it at present exists, and believe that,
while the Eastern Church is a legitimate branch of the
Church Catholic, the non-Episcopal communions of the
West, with their manifold activities, their close contact
with the life and thought of the present day, are outside
the pale? Was the Christian faith more influential,
was the Christian life truer and purer, when the Church
was outwardly one, than it is now?

Some years ago a great authority exhorted politicians
to use maps constructed on a large scale; meaning that
by so doing they would gain a juster view of the true
proportions and relations and boundaries of different
territories. The same advice might well be given to
ecclesiastics. We are too apt to regard Church history
from our own point of view, and to go to it to find
confirmation for our own preconceived theories, rather
than to trace in it the gradual working out of God's
plan, the evolution of His spiritual kingdom. And so,
too, we are apt to confine our view to our own special
territory, till we come to identify this with the Catholic
Church. But as Goethe said, "Hinter dem Berge sind
auch Leute"—there are people beyond the mountains,—
so beyond the hills which stand round about our Jerusalem there are active, intelligent, devout Christian communities, and if we refuse to hold commerce with them,
we shall be doing wrong both to ourselves and to them.

We are brought back, then, to the fundamental ques-

H

tion, What is the true relation of the Christian ministry
to the constitution of the Christian Church? St. Paul,
in the passage to which I have already referred in these
lectures, describes the Jewish priesthood as διάκονοι
γράμματος, the Christian as διάκονοι πνεύματος. The
former would be those who are charged with the
administration of a system written and engraven on
stones. Their ministry would be one of routine; their
ideal would be the formal adherence to a written code.
Such a priesthood is made, to use the language of the
Epistle to the Hebrews, κατὰ νόμον ἐντολῆς σαρκίνης—
after the law of a carnal commandment. The succession
of such a priesthood would be a formal and carnal one.
But the Christian priesthood, being a ministry of the
Spirit, was κατὰ δύναμιν ζωῆς ἀκαταλύτου—after the
power of an endless life. The essence of a minister of
the Old Covenant was that he should be of the family
of Aaron. The essence of a minister of the New
Covenant is, that he should be called of God. And
ordination in the Christian Church is, not the adding
of one more link to the mystic chain through which the
Divine influence is transmitted from the Apostles to
the modern Church, not the empowering a man by
certain ritual acts to convey grace to the people, but
the solemn recognition of the Divine call, the choosing
and calling to the work of the ministry "by men who
have publick authority given unto them in the Congregation, to call and send Ministers into the Lord's
vineyard."

But if this is so, it follows of necessity that the

essence of the Church cannot depend upon the form of the ministry; for then it would be, not of the spirit, but of the letter. The Church does not depend upon the ministry, but rather the ministry upon the Church. That this was the view taken at the Reformation, the view which the English Church distinctly and deliberately accepted and acted upon, I shall endeavour to show in a later lecture;[1] and if at the Restoration in the seventeenth century a different view prevailed, that cannot bind the Church of England for all time to a reactionary theory. We may be thankful that both Episcopacy and monarchy have been retained, and that both in Church and State we possess an organic connection with the past: but we need not therefore condemn those who have seen fit to adopt different ecclesiastical or political organizations; we may recognize a providential design in variety no less than in uniformity. Let us not in our zeal for a theory of Catholicity close our eyes to facts. Set on the one side the saying of Ignatius,[2] that as many as are of God and of Christ, they are with the Bishop; and on the other the patent facts of religious life in the English colonies and in the United States, and shall we say that the teaching of history is to have no weight against the dictum of an Apostolic Father, writing under wholly different circumstances and with a different view? The Divine will is revealed in the course of events as well as in the Scriptures; and if we find that the grace of God is not limited to any outward

[1] See Lecture VIII.
[2] Ignatius, Ep. ad Philadelph., iii.

form or organization, if we find Episcopal Churches, Presbyterian Churches, Congregationalist Churches, not only existing but vindicating their right to exist by fruitful Christian work and by a long and honourable lineage, must we not be led to the conclusion that any system which ignores the existence of this variety, and which, in spite of facts, insists upon so defining the Church as to exclude from its brotherhood a large part of the most energetic and intelligent forms of Christian life, must be defective or erroneous, must need replacing or supplementing by a theory more adequate to the facts? Surely a theory which unites us with the Abyssinian and Coptic Churches because they have Bishops, and separates us from the Wesleyans because they have none, stands self-convicted of unreality; and unreality in religion is a dangerous thing.

What, then, you may ask, are we to be contented with the present disjointed, disorganized condition of Christendom? Are we to accept a boundless sectarianism as the highest achievement of the Christian spirit? To this question I hope to attempt an answer in a later lecture, when I come to speak of the Church of the future. For the present, let us lay to heart this principle, that the Christian ministry is a ministry not of the letter but of the spirit; that it is not, like that of the Old Covenant, a service of outward forms and observances; but that, unless it is quickened and instinct with the Spirit of God, it is naught. Let us settle it in our minds that the ministry is essential to the Church only in the sense that organization is essential to every society ; that what the minister does is the act of the congregation ; and that the highest aim a minister can set before him is to train his people to be independent of him. Let us remember that the true Apostolical succession is a succession not mechanical but spiritual ; that, as Origen says,[1] the prerogative given to St. Peter after the letter belongs according to the spirit to every one who is like St. Peter ; and that, for the present at least, the truest bond of union for the Church of Christ is not a common ministry nor a common form of worship, but a common allegiance to Christ, a unity not outward, not of the letter, but inward and of the spirit.

[1] Origen, In Matt., tom. xii., ed. Caillau : Καὶ εἴ τις λέγει τοῦτο πρὸς αὐτὸν . . . τεύξεται τῶν εἰρημένων, ὡς μὲν τὸ γράμμα τοῦ εὐαγγελίου λέγει, πρὸς ἐκεῖνον τὸν Πέτρον, ὡς δὲ τὸ πνεῦμα αὐτοῦ διδάσκει, πρὸς πάντα τὸν γενόμενον, ὁποῖος ὁ Πέτρος ἐκεῖνος.

LECTURE V.

IN THE SACRAMENTS.

"It is the Spirit that quickeneth; the flesh profiteth nothing: the words that I have spoken unto you are spirit, and are life."— JOHN vi. 63.

THE distinction between the letter and the spirit, between the material and formal, is, as I have already said, one which runs through all religion, and which underlies almost all controversies. If once we could solve the question, with regard to our religious belief and observances, What is the eternal and unchangeable and what is the transitory and accidental element? we should have arrived at the end of disputations, and should be, like Richard Baxter in his later years, "much more inclinable to reconciling principles." It is my earnest desire in these lectures to minister to what, I trust, is a characteristic feature of our time—the tendency to base our religious life, not on the subtleties of controversial theology, but rather on the "reconciling principles" which will endure when the "wood, hay, stubble" which have been built upon them shall be burnt up.

We have seen that St. Paul describes the ministry of the New Covenant as a ministry of the spirit, and that he speaks of Christians as serving God in newness of the

spirit, and not in oldness of the letter. And in so doing
he is only carrying out the principle laid down by our
Lord, that "God is a Spirit, and they that worship Him
must worship Him in spirit and in truth." And from
this principle of the purely spiritual nature of God's
kingdom it would seem to follow of necessity that all
worship must be spiritual; that, as all human life is
redeemed and sanctified by Christ, all times and places
and persons are alike holy, and that in the Christian
system there is no room for days or places or persons
specially set apart for the service of God. In a former
lecture I have quoted a weighty passage from Bishop
Lightfoot's Essay on the " Christian Ministry," in which
this principle is asserted with the utmost lucidity. But,
after laying down this great ideal, the Bishop at once
acknowledges that it is " strictly an *ideal,* which we
must ever hold before our eyes, which should inspire
and interpret ecclesiastical polity, but which nevertheless
cannot supersede the necessary wants of human society,
and, if crudely and hastily applied, will lead only to
signal failure." In truth, a purely spiritual religion is
suited only for purely spiritual beings.[1] If in our religion
we ignore the material side of our nature, that side of
our nature will assuredly assert and avenge itself. And
therefore no religion that has ever existed has been able
to dispense with some kind of ritual. In those which
have attempted it, the very absence of ritual becomes
in itself a kind of traditional form of worship. Hence

[1] Cf. " Baxter's Catechizing of Families," p. 392 : " A soul in flesh
is apt to use sense, and needs some help of it."

in modern Christianity we find, partly by direct institution of Christ, partly as the result of a natural growth under the influence of its surroundings, a system of sacraments, ordinances of worship, forms of Church government, and ecclesiastical customs and traditions, which form, as it were, the embodiment of the Christian spirit, and which, to the minds of most persons, are inseparable from Christianity itself. Still, we must never forget that all these outward things are but accidents, even if they be inseparable accidents, of the kingdom of God; that in its essence that kingdom is independent of them; that it is a Covenant, not of letter, not of outer forms and observances, but of spirit—of the life which comes direct from God; that these things are but means to an end, and that if they are treated as ends in themselves they at once become hindrances to the spiritual kingdom.

Our subject to-day is the letter and the spirit, or the outward and the inward part, in the Sacraments, limiting the use of the term to the two ordinances which are specially recognized as such by the Church of England.

Christ was accustomed to speak of Himself as introducing or revealing a kingdom. " The kingdom of Heaven is likened " unto this or that, is the familiar beginning of His parables as recorded by St. Matthew. But a kingdom denotes persons standing in a certain relation, first, to the king, and, secondly, to each other as fellow-subjects. In other words, to be a disciple of Christ is not merely to accept His teaching; it is to enter into and continue in a certain definite relation to Him and to humanity in Him. And accordingly the only two outward forms which can claim His sanction symbolize, the one admission to, and the other continuance and confirmation in, the Christian society or brotherhood. It is in this sense that St. Paul always appeals to them as witnesses of the corporate life of the Church : "In one Spirit were we all baptized into one body; and were all made to drink of one Spirit;" "The bread which we break, is it not a communion of the body of Christ? seeing that we, who are many, are one bread, one body; for we all partake of the one bread;" "He that eateth and drinketh, eateth and drinketh judgment unto himself, if he discern not the body." Other meanings and other benefits, no doubt, may be found in the Sacraments, but these are the root-ideas out of which all the rest spring. We proceed, then, to discuss each of the Sacraments separately, looking at them in the earliest form in which we find them, and trying to discriminate between that which is of the letter and that which is of the spirit.

The washing of the body with water was a familiar symbol among Oriental nations for the putting off all moral pollution and uncleanness. It was enjoined by the Jewish law as a ceremonial act for the Priests, and for all persons who had contracted ceremonial defilement; and it seems certain that before our Lord's time it had been adopted as part of the ritual for the admission of proselytes into the Jewish Covenant.[1]

[1] Cf. Bishop Harold Browne, in Smith's "Bible Dict.," *s.v.* "Baptism." Winer's "Bibl. Realwörterbuch," *s.v.* "Proselyten."

This simple and expressive action was adopted by John the Baptist for his disciples, and by our Lord as the form of admission into His society ; in each case it was the outward and visible sign of that putting away of past sin and entering with purified heart and conscience upon a new life, which both the one and the other proclaimed.　And after our Lord's departure, it became by His appointment the established form by which new members were admitted to His Church.　To understand what Baptism was and what it involved in the earliest days of the Church, we must remember how entirely it changed a man's whole life.　He had been brought up in one or other of the heathen religions, a worshipper of the gods of Greece or Rome or Egypt; or else he had been a Jew, taught to believe that in Jerusalem was the place where men ought to worship ; or perhaps he had grown up in the philosophical scepticism which had so largely undermined both Jewish and Gentile religion, and had learnt as the highest achievement of wisdom—

" Pacata posse omnia mente tueri." [1]

But he had accepted Christ as his Master and Saviour, and he came to profess his faith in Him.　He pronounced the words, "I renounce thee, Satan ; I join myself to Thee, O Christ."　He was plunged beneath the baptismal water, and he rose up a Christian.　In that water he washed away the stains of his past life. Beneath it he was buried with Christ ; from it he rose to newness of life.　It was hardly a metaphor, it was

[1] Lucretius, v. 1202.

almost a literal fact, to say that he was dead, that he was born again, that he had passed out of darkness into the light, that he had been initiated. He entered upon a new career, among new friends and associates, with new interests, new hopes, new motives, a new and all-pervading affection.

What a complete contrast, to all outward appearance, to modern Baptism ! An unconscious infant is brought to the font, often as a mere concession to custom, often in consequence of much pressure from the clergyman or his agents ; not uncommonly we find persons who do not know whether they have been baptized or not ; very rarely is Baptism thought of by modern Christians as an epoch in their lives. We still keep the old phraseology ; we still give thanks to God that the child is regenerate, we still pray that he "may lead the rest of his life according to this beginning ;" we still teach children to say that in Baptism they were made "members of Christ, the children of God, and inheritors of the kingdom of Heaven ;" but to most persons this language is unreal, it answers to no kind of spiritual fact of which they are conscious. And may we not trace the reason of this in the history of the Church ? When the Christian community was in the first freshness of its new life, when the multitude of them that believed were of one heart and of one soul, when to become a Christian was to be welcomed into a united family, when the Church and the world were so distinct that Christians naturally spoke and thought of the one as darkness, the other as light, then to be baptized was indeed to put on Christ, to be made a member of His body. But gradually, as the simplicity of the Christian life wore off—as the Church became, not the natural and spontaneous union of those who were bound together by a common faith and a common love, but a great super-natural corporation, endowed with mysterious powers for the purpose of saving men's souls from the wrath to come,—Baptism was no longer the simple act by which men professed discipleship to Christ and were admitted to the membership of God's family, but a mystic cere-mony by which the guilt of original sin was washed away, by which the evil spirit dwelling in the natural man was exorcised, by which a mark was impressed and grace infused into the soul, by which one born under a curse was reconciled to God. The simple and natural terms which had formerly been used to express the greatness of the change involved in coming out of heathen life into the communion of the Christian Church —regeneration, enlightenment, initiation, sealing,—were regarded no longer as metaphors, but as literal expres-sions of a mysterious inward change wrought by contact with the water and the uttering of the prescribed words. Infants were brought to be baptized, not as the joyful and thankful recognition of the fact of God's universal love, not as a visible declaration of the brotherhood in which Christ had united all mankind, but to save them from those everlasting fires to which all who died with-out Baptism were doomed.[1] And lest any should through

[1] Augustine (Contra Julianum, III.) says of an unbaptized infant, "Quid miraris in igne æterno cum diabolo futurum, qui in

difficulty or misadventure be left to so dreadful a fate,
it was mercifully provided that Baptism might be
administered, not only in the congregation or by those
to whom it pertained officially to administer the discipline and sacraments of the Church, but in any place,
by any person, man or woman.   So that the initiatory
act whereby originally converts from heathenism—and
then, in full accordance with the spirit at least of the
New Covenant, infants—were brought into organic union
with the body of Christ, the Christian society, became
little better than a magical incantation, whereby the
Divine favour was procured and the designs of Satan
frustrated.

We can hardly wonder that in different directions
men should have revolted against the hardness of the
letter and striven after something more spiritual.   Baptism, said one class of persons, professes to be the
entrance into the kingdom of Heaven ; but to enter that
kingdom needs repentance and faith ; surely, then, the
only proper subjects of Baptism are not infants, but
persons capable of repentance and faith.   Surely the
only profession of discipleship is that which is made
with full knowledge and deliberate choice ; is it not
more reasonable to wait until persons are of age to
choose for themselves whether they will be Christ's disciples or not ?   On the other hand, another class of
persons maintained that, the kingdom of Christ being

Dei regnum intrare non sinitur ? "   Elsewhere, indeed (De Pecca-
torum Meritis, i.), he says, " Potest proinde recte dici, parvulos sine
baptismo de corpore exeuntes in *damnatione omnium levissima* futuros."

purely spiritual, the only Baptism that was needed was that of the Spirit ; that the water was a mere temporary symbol which the Church in its maturity might safely dispense with. And nearer to our own day, when an excessive individualism has proclaimed that a man's religion is entirely a matter between himself and his God, and when the corporate character of Christianity has been overlooked, Baptism has been reduced to an edifying ceremony wherein believing parents offered their children to God.[1]

We shall not be able to meet the arguments either of the Baptist or of the Quaker, until we have risen to a higher and wider conception of what that society is to which Baptism admits us. If Baptism is the door of entrance to a denomination, if we bring children to be baptized in order that they may adopt this or that set of opinions, or this or that form of worship, then undoubtedly it would be reasonable that we should give them an opportunity of choosing for themselves what their religion shall be or whether they will have any religion. Or if Baptism is set forth to us as a charm to deliver us from the punishment of the sin of Adam, then we could understand men thinking that it might be a less evil to dispense with the outward washing altogether than to have recourse to it as a means of rescuing children from the wrath of their heavenly Father. But if we will open our minds to the truth that God's

[1] It is said that among English Congregationalists Baptism is falling into increasing neglect. Indeed, it is not easy to see how it fits in with their Church theories.

will is to sum up all things in Christ, the things in the
heavens and the things upon the earth; if we will learn
to believe in the Holy Catholic Church, in no restricted
or narrow sense, but as the firstfruits and the representative of the great human brotherhood; if we will
remember that Baptism means, not that we have chosen
Christ, but that He has chosen us; then it will become
to us full of life and meaning, and we shall see in it, not
a mere edifying ceremony, nor yet a means of averting
Divine wrath, but the declaration to each child of God's
Fatherhood, the incorporation of a new member into
that society which Christ founded upon earth to be the
nucleus of a great world-wide brotherhood, in which His
Spirit should dwell, and by which mankind should be
edified into conformity with the Divine plan.

More than half the controversies and misunderstand-
ings which have arisen in the Church have been the
result of interpreting metaphors literally. By Baptism
a person was introduced into a new world of spiritual
influences, just as by birth he had been introduced into
a new world of physical influences. There was an
obvious analogy between the beginnings of the natural
and of the spiritual life. What then could be more
fitting than to speak of the Sacrament whereby an infant
or an adult was brought into contact with the life which
circulated in the Christian society as a new birth? But
when this simple and expressive metaphor of regeneration was interpreted after the letter, Baptism came to
be looked upon as a charm by which a mysterious
inward change was wrought in the unconscious soul, and

men taught that, though concupiscence remained, yet it was mitigated and diminished by baptismal grace ; that the Spirit moves upon the face of the waters of Baptism, and sanctifies them so that they receive power to sanctify.

> " A few calm words of faith and prayer,
> A few bright drops of holy dew,
> Shall work a wonder there
> Earth's charmers never knew."

Who does not see that in all this we have rhetoric mistaken for logic, images of spiritual things substituted for the spiritual truths which they represent ? And if we would restore the Sacrament of Baptism to its rightful position as the initiation into the spiritual world, we must make the Christian society more real, more Catholic ; we must see that that into which persons are baptized is not a mere religious denomination, but in some measure at least the kingdom of Heaven upon earth. It is true that always the solemnities of religion represent rather the ideal than the actual; it is right that we should use the glowing words of the Baptismal Office to set forth the great heritage to which all alike are called, even when we have a sorrowful consciousness in the particular case that there is little likelihood of the child being brought up to lead the rest of his life according to this beginning ; but we must at the same time remember that it is only by rising out of the literal into the spiritual that we can make Baptism a reality of the religious life.

The most striking and interesting instance of the

relation of the letter to the spirit is undoubtedly to be found in that great central ordinance of Christianity which can be regarded under many aspects, and is called by many names, the Lord's Supper, the Holy Communion, the Eucharist, the Mass. Let us look for a moment at the contrasts which under its extreme forms it presents to us.

In the earliest detailed account of the celebration of the Lord's Supper, that given by Justin Martyr, we cannot fail to be struck with the fact that what is described is a social feast, a popular religious solemnity, conducted according to an accepted type, yet not without a certain element of spontaneity, consisting of the offering of praise and thanksgiving and of the fruits of the earth, of the consecration of bread and of wine mixed with water by the presiding brother,[1] who offers up prayers and thanksgivings according to his power;[2] of the partaking of the consecrated elements by the assembled people, and of the sending portions to those who are absent. As we advance, the traces of fixed liturgical forms become increasingly clear : but everywhere the popular element is conspicuous; it is always, "We pray," "We give thanks," "We offer sacrifices." And with this agree the slight and informal notices in the Acts of the Apostles and the First Epistle to the Corinthians. "The brethren came together to break bread." "The bread which we break; the cup which

---

[1] Προσφέρεται τῷ προεστῶτι τῶν ἀδελφῶν ἄρτος, καὶ ποτήριον ὕδατος καὶ κράματος.—Just. Mart., Apol., 2.

[2] Ὅση δύναμις αὐτῷ.—L.c.

I

we bless." "We, the many, are one bread, one body."

If a Christian of the second century could return to life and be present at a Low Mass of the Roman Church, at which there may or may not be worshippers present, at which no one but the Priest communicates, at which no sound of a voice is heard, and from which the social element is quite absent, would it occur to his mind that what he saw represented the familiar ceremony in which he had been accustomed to take part ? It would be a bold assertion to make. Nay, are we quite sure that in any Church throughout Christendom—Greek, Roman, Anglican, Lutheran, Presbyterian, Congregationalist, Methodist—he would see what would recall to him the Eucharistic Feast of the early Church ?

If this is so—if in this great central act of worship the variations have been so great ; if the Ordinance of a rural congregation English of Nonconformists and the Pontifical High Mass of St. Peter's at Rome both claim as their origin the acts and words of Christ on the night before His Passion, both profess to be that perpetual memory of His Death which He commanded us to continue until His coming again, it may be well to see whether under this outward diversity any substratum of unity exists,—whether, if we trace the Eucharist up to its Source, we can find a permanent, unchanging principle which is the same in all ages and in all Churches.

The earliest documentary evidence we possess referring to the Eucharist is, of course, the mention of

it in 1 Cor. x. and xi. : the latter chapter containing
an account of its institution, which St. Paul says he
received of the Lord, and which is evidently akin to
the narrative in St. Luke's Gospel. The other two
synoptic Gospels have a parallel though independent
narrative. From these we gather that, on the night
when our Lord ate His last Passover with His disciples,
He engrafted upon the traditional feast of the Old
Covenant a new observance. He took bread—the unleavened Paschal cake—"and when He had given
thanks, He brake it, and said, This is My body,
which is for you : this do in remembrance of Me." And
after supper He took the cup of blessing, which formed
part of the traditional observance though not of the
original institution of the Passover, saying, "This cup
is the New Covenant in My blood : this do, as oft as ye
drink it, in remembrance of Me. For as often as ye eat
this bread, and drink the cup, ye proclaim the Lord's
death till He come." On this simple narrative we may
remark, first, that the Lord's Supper, like His kingdom,
had its roots in the Old Covenant. He used the same
elements which, though only accessory to the Passover,
had yet served for the Paschal meal. He passed by the
lamb, which was the essential element, and took the
unleavened bread, which was a part though not the
central or characteristic part of the feast, and the cup
of wine mixed with water, which was a mere social
addition, and He calls the bread His body, and the cup
the New Covenant in His blood: alluding evidently
to the blood of the Covenant with which Moses had

sprinkled the people before he went up into the mount.[1]
And this bread and this cup, which He thus identified
with Himself, He told His disciples to eat and drink in
remembrance of Him, and with reference (as St. Paul
adds) to His coming again, or (according to St. Matthew
and St. Mark) to the day when He should drink it new
with them in His Father's kingdom.

But the phenomena of the fourth Gospel in this
connection are very remarkable. The Passover, which
the Synoptists identify with the meal eaten on the
night before the Crucifixion, is relegated by the fourth
Evangelist to the day following that event. And though
a discourse pronounced on the Thursday evening is re-
ported at great length, yet no allusion whatever is made
to the institution of the Eucharist. But, on the other
hand, at a much earlier period of our Lord's ministry,
St. John records a discourse delivered just before an
earlier Passover, the phraseology of which coincides in
a remarkable manner with the language attributed to our
Lord by the Synoptists in connection with the Eucharist.
In the discourse at Capernaum after the feeding of the
five thousand,[2] our Lord speaks of Himself as the
Bread of Life, and adds, "He that cometh to Me shall
never hunger, and he that believeth on Me shall never
thirst." And He further says, "The bread which I will
give is My flesh, which I will give for the life of the
world." And when the Jews strove one with another,
saying, "How can this Man give us His flesh to eat?"
Jesus said, "Except ye eat the flesh of the Son of Man,

---

[1] Exod. xxiv. 8.   [2] John vi.

and drink His blood, ye have not life in yourselves. He
that eateth My flesh and drinketh My blood hath eternal
life ; and I will raise him up at the last day. For My
flesh is meat indeed, and My blood is drink indeed."

If we accept both the discourse in St. John and the
synoptic narrative of the Supper as authentic, it is
impossible to suppose that they are not in some way
related to each other. If Christ spoke of eating His
flesh and drinking His blood as a necessity of the
spiritual life, and afterwards, at a solemn moment of
His life, said, "Take, eat, this is My body ; and drink
ye all of this, for this is My blood," it seems plain that
the one utterance could not have been made without
reference to the other, and we may reasonably suppose
that the one is to be interpreted by the other. But the
important question is, which is to be interpreted by the
other ? Are we to say that the discourse at Capernaum
was a dark saying, of which the disciples were not
intended to understand the meaning until it was made
clear by the words and acts of the Paschal Supper, or
was Christ in the discourse laying down a great spiritual
truth, which, if the disciples had received it into their
minds and understandings, would have enabled them at
once to recognize His meaning in the institution of the
Eucharist ?

Let us look more closely at the words of the discourse
in John vi.

Our Lord saw that the multitude who had followed
Him across the lake were actuated by no higher motive
than a desire to get what He might be able and willing

to bestow; and so He exhorts them to work, not for the meat which perisheth, but for the meat which abideth unto everlasting life. The mention of work led them to suppose that some efforts of their own could obtain the gift He spoke of; and they asked, "What must we do that we may work the works of God?" He tells them that it is not a question of working, but of believing: "This is the work of God, that ye believe on Him Whom He hath sent." And when they asked for a sign, and spoke of the manna which Moses had given the people from heaven, He declared, "It was not Moses that gave you the bread out of heaven; but My Father giveth you the true bread out of heaven. For the bread of God is that which cometh down out of heaven and giveth life unto the world." And he added, "I am the bread of life: he that cometh to Me shall not hunger; and he that believeth on Me shall never thirst."

So far there is little difficulty in understanding the general meaning. The people were following Him from a low, carnal motive; they desired such food as Moses had brought out of heaven. But Christ's object was not to satisfy their bodily hunger, nor yet to impress their imagination by wonderful works, but to supply their spiritual needs. Accordingly, just as He had spoken to the Samaritan woman at Jacob's well of living water springing up within a man unto everlasting life, so here he tries to raise the thoughts and desires of the people to a higher and more spiritual level by speaking of Himself as the bread of life. What they really needed was nourishment for their spiritual life; and that nourishment

they could receive by believing on Him, the living
bread, Who had life in Himself, Who had come that
they might have life, and have it more abundantly.
But, after this, a new scene seems to open.   The Jews—
no longer the multitude, but the Jews, "the representa-
tives of the dominant religious party"[1]—"murmured
concerning Him because He said, I am the bread
which came down out of heaven."   And, after repeating
His previous declaration that He is the bread of life, He
tells them that the bread which He will give is His flesh,
which He will give for the life of the world.   Here, with
the word "flesh" comes in for the first time the sug-
gestion of His death.   And then He speaks of eating
His flesh and drinking His blood as the condition of
having eternal life.   Here, surely, is a declaration that
it is by receiving Him, His life-giving Spirit, into themselves, by being made conformable to His death, that
they can be nourished to life eternal.   Does He give
any hint that this is a mystery which would not be
made known to them till long afterwards, when He
would be about to leave them ?   Far from it.   He speaks
of the present.   "He that eateth My flesh and drinketh
My blood hath eternal life, and I will raise him up
[will perfect him] at the last day."   And, as though to
meet and obviate any gross and carnal understanding of
His words, when His disciples complained, "This is a
hard saying; who can hear it ?" He said, "It is the spirit
that quickeneth ; the flesh profiteth nothing : the words
that I have spoken unto you are spirit, and are life."

[1] Westcott on St. John, p. 104.

There are, as I have said, two possible lines of interpretation of this great passage. If we say that it refers
to the sacramental feeding on Christ's body and blood in
the Eucharist, and that our Lord was speaking by anticipation of a rite which He intended to institute, probably
a year later, we are substituting the letter for the spirit,
the outward for the inward. In the weighty words of
Dr. Westcott, "The teaching . . . treats essentially of
spiritual realities, with which no external act, as such,
can be co-extensive. . . . To attempt to transfer the
words of the discourse with their consequences to the
Sacrament is not only to involve the history in hopeless
confusion, but to introduce overwhelming difficulties into
their interpretation." On the other hand, the spiritual
reference of the passage is well brought out in the well-
known words of St. Augustine, "Believe and thou hast
eaten;" and in those of St. Bernard, "To eat His flesh
and drink His blood, what is it but to be partakers of His
sufferings and to imitate His conversation which He
had in the flesh?" Indeed, the relation of the Sacrament to the discourse cannot be more tersely expressed
than in the words of St. Augustine in reference to Christ
as the bread which came down from heaven:[1] "Hunc

---

[1] Aug., in Joh. Evan., xxvi. § 12. In the text of the
Benedictine edition the words are "Hunc panem *significavit* Altare
Dei." But in a note we read, "MSS. plerique *significat*." The
perfect tense would make it refer to the Jewish Altar. But
"Altare Dei" is Augustine's familiar title for the Christian Altar,
and the change of tense is one which the monkish copyist would
be likely to make, lest St. Augustine should seem to speak of the
Eucharist as *signifying* and not *being* the Bread of Life.

In connexion with Augustine's view of the Eucharist, there

panem significavit manna, hunc panem significat altare
Dei." The discourse and the Sacrament alike have
reference to the same spiritual reality, the inward feeding
on Christ by faith, the receiving nourishment and
strength from Him, the transfusion of His Spirit into us.
To find in the discourse an exposition of the doctrine
of the Sacrament is—in the words of Meyer—an unex-
ampled and inconceivable ὕστερον πρότερον. The earlier
Christian writers no doubt apply the phraseology of
the discourse to the Eucharist: but it is remarkable
that, while using the strongest possible language, language sometimes overstepping the limits of sober reverence, of the eating and drinking of the body and blood
of Christ in the Sacrament, they yet seem always conscious that it is figurative language that they are using.
Origen applies St. Paul's words about the letter and the
spirit to this subject.[1] "There is," he says, "in the
Gospels too a letter, which kills him who understands not
spiritually the things which are spoken. For if thou
followest out according to the letter this very saying,
'Except ye eat My flesh and drink My blood,' this letter

is a curious story in his third book "Contra Julianum," how one
Acatius, a contemporary of his own, had been born with his
eyes closed, and how, when he was five years old, his mother had
succeeded in opening them, *imposito ex Eucharistia cataplasmate.* It
is difficult to understand this of anything but the consecrated bread
of the Eucharist; but if so, it implies a view of the Sacrament
singularly remote from any modern theory.

[1] "Est enim et in evangeliis littera, quæ occidit eum, qui non
spiritaliter, quæ dicuntur, adverterit. Si enim secundum litteram
sequaris hoc ipsum, quod dictum est: Nisi manducaveritis carnem
meam et biberitis sanguinem meum, occidit hæc littera."—Hom.
viii. 5, in Lev.

killeth." And St. Augustine warns us to honour the
Sacraments, not in slavishness of the flesh, but in freedom of the spirit. And to take the sign for the thing
signified he [1] calls a mark of "servilis infirmitas."

It is strange how largely the letter has superseded
the spirit in the doctrine of the Lord's Supper. Selden's
pithy saying of the doctrine of transubstantiation, [2]
"That opinion is only Rhetoric turned into Logic," contains briefly the history of sacramental dogma. "Without a parable spake He not unto them" is the Evangelist's
account of our Lord's teaching to the multitude. And
the one Evangelist who gives us no parables properly so
called, records a number of parabolic sayings which we
must take into account if we would understand His
method. "I am the Door;" "I am the Good Shepherd;"
"I am the Vine;" "I am the Bread of Life;"—all these
sayings set forth Christ in His relation to His people
under various aspects. They show how natural it was
to Him to use the things of sense for expressing spiritual
truths. And the image of eating and drinking, of
inwardly digesting, was a very familiar one to his
hearers. "Come, eat of My bread, and drink of the
wine which I have mingled," is the invitation of
Wisdom in the Book of Proverbs. But in the case of the
Eucharist there is a further and a deeper significance.
For Christ goes on to say, "The bread which I will give
is My flesh, which I will give for the life of the world."
He was indeed a Teacher sent from God, and if He had

---

[1] Aug., De Doct. Christ., III. 9.
[2] Selden's "Table Talk."

said simply, " I am the bread of life," we should have
accepted it as a claim that we should receive and
assimilate His doctrine ; but when He speaks of giving
His flesh for the life of the world, it is clear that He
points to His Incarnation and Sacrifice as the life-giving
food of His people.   So far, then, it is quite true that
the discourse at Capernaum contained a mystery which
the hearers could not yet fully comprehend.   But the
main point is, that the discourse was not a prophecy of
the Lord's Supper, but the Supper was the precipitating
and fixing in visible and tangible signs of that which
Christ had already given as a spiritual revelation to His
disciples.

That He should thus have embodied the relation
between Himself and His people in a visible action is a
signal proof of His insight into human nature.   Not
only because—

> "Segnius irritant animos demissa per aurem,
> Quam quæ sunt oculis subjecta fidelibus ; "

but also because an institution or an observance gathers
round itself a history of its own, and gives fresh significance and vitality to the doctrine which it enshrines.
In truth, the history of the Eucharist would be to a
great extent a history of the inner life of Christendom.
It has influenced, and in its turn been influenced by,
the course of Church life.   In the New Testament we
find it in its primitive simplicity: at Troas, the midnight
celebration in the upper chamber ; at Corinth, the Lord's
Supper and the Love-feast almost indistinguishably
blended.   But soon new elements appear : we see the

separation of the Communion from the Love-feast; the transition from the late evening to the early morning; the development of the idea of sacrifice—first the thank-offering of the fruits of the earth, then the offering of themselves by the people as a reasonable, holy, and lively sacrifice; then the solemn commemoration of the sacrifice of Christ; and finally the propitiatory sacrifice of the Mass: we see the growth of the idea of communion, first with the persons present signified by the kiss of peace, then with absent brethren, then with the dead, and the mention by name of departed saints: parallel with this, the growth of the sacerdotal aspect of the Sacrament, so that it is no longer The bread which we the Christian congregation, but The bread which we the Priests break; the change from the primitive Basilica arrangement, in which the Bishop, descending from his throne at the eastern extremity of the Church, stood behind the Holy Table with his face towards the people; the development of the simple apsidal termination into the deep chancel and the elaborate sanctuary, so that the very architecture of our mediæval churches bears testimony to the changed aspect of the worship for which they were built: we see the whole institution gradually transformed from the simple act of communion with Christ and with His people into a gorgeous pageant, an awful mystery, the worship of Christ present on the Altar. But through all it has been a perpetual memory of the sacrifice of the death of Christ; under the utmost variety of forms it has shown forth the Lord's death. And when the Reformation came, and with it the restoration of the simpler and purer idea of Christian worship, the Eucharist reverted in the Protestant Churches to something like its earlier type, and the Mass gave way to the Communion, and the spirit once more asserted itself as superior to the letter.

It may at first seem startling, when we discover that the great central usage of Christianity, that which our Lord appointed to be observed in memory of Him until His coming again, should have so varied from age to age, and that it should have been made the central position of the battle of the Reformation. It is startling, if we think chiefly of the outward form, and not of the inward spirit. But we must remember that the condition on which an observance exists is that it should so adapt itself as to be intelligible to and in contact with the inner life of varying generations; and that the simple coming together of the brethren to break bread, natural and expressive as it was to men accustomed to the social life of the synagogue, could hardly supersede the more sensuous worship of the Greek, the Roman, and the Teuton, until it had drawn to itself something of the element of awe and mystery. We know how even at Corinth the Holy Feast was made a scene of revelry and excess; probably in a ruder age and country it was necessary to sacrifice altogether the social in order to preserve the religious aspect of the Sacrament. It is of the very essence of Christianity that forms are non-essential and variable; even Sacraments ordained by Christ have preserved their spirit only by modification of the letter. And this being so, it becomes a question of deep importance, What is to be the relation of the Eucharist to the changing social conditions of the present age ?

If we watch the signs of the times, we cannot doubt that the great social idea which this age is destined to carry out is that of the solidarity of mankind. The motto of the French Revolution, "Freedom, Equality, Brotherhood," though its brightness was quenched in clouds of war and despotism, was yet a true expression of the need of the age. It is in this direction, if at all, that humanity must advance. And if the Christian Church has no message to deliver on this matter, we cannot wonder if men ignore her, and turn for help to other teachers. If, indeed, Christianity had been, as some of its advocates have tried to make it, a religion of the letter,—if, that is to say, it had been tied down to a certain set of political dogmas, or had been the advocate of aristocracy against democracy, of privilege against equality, it would by this time have been a mere survival, waxing old and ready to vanish away. It is true that the Church has not always risen to the height of her Divine Charter, and has sometimes timidly sought the alliance of this or that political party, and has shrunk from adapting herself to new social conditions and to the needs of new classes. And where she has thus fallen short of her possibilities, she has learnt by bitter experience to rue her mistake. But all the time in her great central Ordinance she has had within her the corrective to her timidity. In the Communion of the Body and Blood of Christ she has the outward expression of her Lord's words, "One is your Master, even Christ, and all ye are brethren." And whatever other and more mysterious significance this Sacrament may have for individual believers, we can hardly doubt that for the Church at large this is what needs most to be insisted on. What is wanted in our perplexed and distracted age is, a simple faith in Christ as the Teacher, the Guide, the Saviour of mankind, and a true sense of brotherhood among all classes and conditions of men. It is true that a large and influential section of the Christian Church insists upon the literal and (if I may say so without offence) the carnal view of the Eucharist as an essential article of the Christian faith. That the validity of each Eucharist depends on the right transmission of Apostolic orders through the Episcopate to the celebrating Priest; that when a rightly ordained Priest pronounces the words of Consecration, Christ becomes then and there present on the Altar; that the virtue of His Incarnation is conveyed to the communicants in and through the bread and wine, and that the bread may be rightly called the Body, and the wine the Blood of Christ;—these are doctrines consistent, no doubt, with the letter of Christ's words, "This is My Body, This is My Blood of the New Covenant," but hardly consistent with the spirit of His teaching. And be it remembered that in this matter we are shut up to the direct declarations of the Lord Himself. No ecclesiastical tradition, no decrees of councils, can have any weight in a question which depends wholly on the

intention of the original institution.   And He Himself
has told us that the flesh profiteth nothing, and that it
is the spirit that giveth life.   He Himself has told us
that it is not in physical nearness to Him, but in hearing
the Word of God and keeping it, that true blessedness
consists.   He Himself has told us that it is expedient
for us that His bodily presence should be withdrawn, in
order that His spiritual presence may be with us.   And
that presence is not dependent on or confined to any
outward rite or any material elements ; it is a presence
which is with us always, and the Sacrament is but the
concentrating and expressing in outward form that real
Presence which pervades the Christian life.   In the
words of Cranmer, " The presence of Christ in His Holy
Supper is a spiritual presence ; and as He is spiritually
present, so is He spiritually eaten of all faithful Christian
men, not only when they receive the Sacrament, but
continually, so long as they be members spiritual of
Christ's mystical body. . . . And as the Holy Ghost
doth not only come to us in Baptism, and Christ doth
there clothe us, but They do the same to us continually
so long as we dwell in Christ ; so likewise doth Christ
feed us so long as we dwell in Him and He in us, and
not only when we receive the Sacrament." [1]

We ask, then, what is that permanent essential
element in the Eucharist, which underlies all varieties
of outward form and all differences of dogmatic view,
and which may be called its Catholic character ?   It is
the expression, first, of that absolute spiritual union with

---

[1] Cranmer's Works, ed. Jenkyns, vol. iii., p. 131.

Christ in which true discipleship consists; secondly, of that brotherly union with our fellow-men, of which the common partaking of the same food is so natural and universal a symbol ; thirdly, of that spirit of sacrifice which found its perfect and eternal expression in the Sacrifice of the Cross ; fourthly, of the looking forward to that new and better world which Christ indicated when He spoke of drinking new wine with His disciples in the kingdom of God. If we thus regard the Holy Communion, we can afford to pass by all metaphysical theories of the manner of Christ's presence as simply unmeaning and nugatory. For indeed, even if our Lord and Saviour were in any local sense present in the elements, what would such a presence profit us ? If we should say, " Blessed are the eyes which see Thee, the hands which handle Thee, the lips which receive Thee, in the Sacrament of Thy Body and Blood," surely He would reply as He did of old, "Yea rather, blessed are they that hear the word of God and keep it." And let us not fear lest in accepting the simpler and more spiritual aspect of the Sacrament we lose any of its true value. We need not lay aside anything of our reverence for Christ's presence because we do not direct that reverence to the material symbols of His presence ; we need not shrink from using the strong language of the ancient hymn—

> " Ecce panis angelorum,
> Factus cibus viatorum,
> Vere panis filiorum,"

if we adopt also the language of St. Augustine : [1] " Fi-

[1] Aug., De Doct. Christ., III. 16.

K

gura est, præcipiens passioni Dominicæ communicandum et suaviter atque utiliter recolendum in memoria quod pro nobis caro ejus crucifixa et vulnerata sit." It is true that, as in the case of Scripture so in the case of the Sacraments, even the superstitious, even the carnal use of them has quickened and nourished many a Christian soul; but no less have Christian souls been quickened and nourished by the simplest remembrance of Christ's death, by the simplest act of communion and fellowship.

> " The Holy Supper is kept indeed,
> In whatso we share with another's need." [1]

Not only in solemn seasons of worship, not only in venerable sanctuaries, but at all times and in all places do Christ's words hold good, " I am the Bread of Life ; he that cometh to Me shall not hunger, and he that believeth on Me shall never thirst."

[1] Lowell, " The Vision of Sir Launfal."

LECTURE VI.

IN CREEDS AND CONFESSIONS OF FAITH.

" We serve in newness of the spirit, and not in oldness of the letter."—Rom. vii. 6 (R.V.).

" It is the Spirit that beareth witness, because the Spirit is the truth."—1 John v. 7 (R.V.).

OUR subject to-day is, The Letter and the Spirit in relation to Christian Creeds and Confessions of Faith.

Before entering upon this subject, it will be well to consider shortly, What do we mean by religion? A man's religion is usually understood to mean that outward profession of faith and those outward observances by which he is united to those who, by a modern barbarism, are called his co-religionists, and is separated from others. And the tendency since the Reformation has undoubtedly been, to make religion more a badge of separation than a basis of union. But in our day this subject has begun to present itself in a new light. As the science of language has taught us to see affinities where, until recently, men only saw diversities, so the science of religion—a science which, as yet, professes to be only in its infancy—is teaching us that beneath all the outward manifestations of religion lies that which is anterior to all religions, the faculty of aspiring and yearning after the Infinite. Not, indeed, that the recognition of this faculty is a new thing; it is what St. Paul expressed in his speech on the Areopagus, when he said that God had made men dependent on Him that they might seek for God, if haply they might feel after Him and find Him; it is what the Psalmist meant when he said, "Such knowledge is too wonderful for me; I cannot attain unto it. Whither shall I go from Thy Spirit? or whither shall I flee from Thy presence?" But it is only now that men are beginning to acknowledge that a true and unhesitating faith in Christ is not incompatible with the belief that, as in the material so in the spiritual world, God is always and everywhere at work, and that men who, in whatever age and under whatever variety of form, have reared altars to an unknown God, have ignorantly worshipped Him Who made the world and all things therein, the Lord of heaven and earth. Certainly we who believe that God has given us eternal life in His Son, need not shrink from acknowledging that He has revealed Himself πολυμερῶς καὶ πολυτρόπως to men who—

> "Stretch lame hands of faith, and grope,
>   And gather dust and chaff, and call
>   To what they feel is Lord of all;"[1]

that Christ is the Son of Man in this sense too, that to Him all the inarticulate yearnings, all the half-conscious questionings of mankind point; that all the thoughts of men about what is higher than themselves, so far as

---

[1] Tennyson, "In Memoriam."

they were not mere perversions and reflections from the light of their own fire, and from the sparks which they have kindled, find their interpretation in Him in Whom are hid all the treasures of wisdom and knowledge.

It is well that this aspect of the subject should not be overlooked in Oxford. In years gone by, theology was regarded as the queen of sciences—"omnium disciplinarum suprema et dignissima."[1] If she is ever to reconquer her position, it must be by claiming a wider territory, by interpreting the meaning of all those varied forms under which men have vaguely guessed at the Infinite, of all those faint visions which they have had of that eternal and invisible world which was above them and about them and within them. As it is impossible to understand Christianity without the aid of Judaism, so it is impossible adequately to comprehend the spirit of religion without the study of those great Eastern beliefs which have influenced so vast a proportion of the human race, nay without some knowledge of those ruder guesses at the great enigma which simpler races have made in the childhood of the world. It has been often pointed out, that for missionaries the very first step in their preparation should be a candid and sympathetic study of the religious beliefs of those to whom they are to be sent, and that they should approach those beliefs in the spirit of our Lord's words, "I am not come to destroy, but to fulfil." But surely for all religious teachers and inquirers it would be a great gain that they should be interested in other

[1] Sanderson, "Logic."

departments of religious thought besides their own, and
that they should learn St. Augustine's lesson,[1] that a
true Christian must understand. that truth belongs to
his Master wherever he finds it. We are all too apt to
think that the Word of God came to us only. We
forget that, if ours is, as we profess, the Catholic
religion, it must gather up as it were into one focus all
the scattered rays of light which come down from the
Father of lights, and that the pure and colourless light
is that which is composed of many blended rays.

And moreover the science of religion teaches us
that theology is not a deductive and stationary, but an
inductive and progressive science. The prevalent conception of theology has been that of a stately temple,
of which the ground-plan has been laid down from the
beginning, and which has been built up gradually by
succeeding generations, each adding something in its
own special style, yet all so as to harmonize with the
general design. And where any reconstruction has been
found necessary, it has been because the builders have
deserted the original foundation, or have built hastily
or with bad materials. But would it not be a truer and
a grander figure to speak of theology as an organism, a
living body, growing and expanding according to the
law of its being, shedding from time to time such rudimentary parts as were not needed for its maturer
functions, adapting itself to its changing environment,

---

[1] "De Doct. Christ.," ii. 18 : " Quisquis bonus verusque Christi-
anus est, Domini sui esse intelligat ubique [? ubicunque] invenerit
veritatem."

preserving its identity, not by the rigid uniformity of inanimate matter, but by the ever-fresh growth and development of organic life? Are not the conditions of all knowledge such, that the goal of one age is the starting-point of another; that what seemed to one generation final and perfect is seen by another to be but partial and provisional, and that the claim of finality is, in fact, an acknowledgment of sterility? All human knowledge, even of things Divine, is imperfect, and therefore capable of progress; and progress involves not only the acceptance of the new, but also the reconsideration and possible reconstruction of the old.

> " Man therefore, thus conditioned, must expect
> He could not, what he knows now, know at first;
> What he considers that he knows to-day,
> Come but to-morrow, he will find misknown;
> Getting increase of knowledge, since he learns
> Because he lives, which is to be a man,
> Set to instruct himself by his past self.
>
>   *   *   *   *   *
>
> God's gift was that man should conceive of truth,
> And yearn to gain it, catching at mistake,
> As midway help till he reach fact indeed.
> The statuary, ere he mould a shape,
> Boasts a like gift, the shape's idea, and next
> The aspiration to produce the same;
> So, taking clay, he calls his shape thereout,
> Cries ever, ' Now I have the thing I see;'
> Yet all the while goes changing what was wrought,
> From falsehood like the truth, to truth itself." [1]

We turn, then, to the subject of the Letter and the Spirit in relation to creeds and confessions of faith.

I have already had occasion to remark upon the fact,

[1] Browning, " A Death in the Desert."

that the earliest Christians not only possessed no sacred writings of their own, but could not even have conceived the possibility of such writings springing up. To them, the end seemed very near; what need could there be of written records for a generation which had seen the Lord when He was on earth, and which hoped to see Him again, coming in the clouds of heaven?

And if there was no need of written records, still less, surely, of formal statements of belief. Why profess a belief in God the Father Almighty, when in seeing Christ they had seen the Father? Why confess that Jesus Christ His only Son had been born, had suffered, had died, had risen again, had gone up into heaven, when they themselves were eye-witnesses of these things? Why say that they believed in the Holy Spirit, when they saw the work of the Spirit everywhere around them, and heard His voice in their hearts? It was superfluous to profess belief in that which they had seen and heard, which they had looked upon and their hands had handled. But the case was different with regard to the reception of new members into the Christian society. Here the traditional formula of admission was itself the framework of a confession of faith; and it was obviously nugatory to admit persons into the Church without some formal assurance that they believed on the Name into which they were baptized. An early writer describes Baptism thus:[1] "Thou wast asked, 'Dost thou believe in God the Father Almighty?'

[1] Pseud. Ambros., "De Sacramentis," bk. ii., c. 7. Quoted in Smith's "Dict. of Eccl. Antiq.," i. 490.

Thou saidst, 'I believe,' and thou wast immersed. Again thou wast asked, 'Dost thou believe also in our Lord Jesus Christ and His Cross?' Thou saidst again, 'I believe,' and wast immersed. A third time thou wast asked, 'Dost thou believe in the Holy Spirit?' Thou didst reply, 'I believe,' and a third time thou wast immersed." Here we have the Baptismal formula expanded into a creed. It is not till the sixth century[1] that we find clear evidence of creeds being used in public worship, and then—as we might expect—it is at the celebration of the Eucharist, as a proof that those who had made profession of their faith at their Baptism continued in it grounded and settled. The practice of using the creed in public worship seems to have arisen in the East, as indeed we might infer from the fact that it is the Eastern form of creed that we now recite in the Communion Service.

But gradually creeds and confessions of faith assumed another aspect. As controversies arose, many of them on vital points, it was natural that councils should be held to determine what was the belief of the Church; and the decisions of such councils were of necessity formulated as authentic records. So that confessions of faith became no longer the simple formulas in which admission to the Christian Church was sought or adherence to the faith professed; they bear the marks of keen discussion, and almost every word of them is molten in the fire of controversy. At the Reformation,

[1] Not till the Third Council of To'edo, A.D. 589. Cf. Lumby's "Hist. of Creeds," p. 101.

the same tendency to precise definition of doctrine prevailed; but now, confessions and articles of religion,
instead of being professedly the embodiment of the
faith of the Church at large, became the distinctive
symbols of particular communions : and the Helvetic,
the Augsburg, the Saxon, the Belgic Confession, the
English Thirty-nine Articles, and the Tridentine Profession of Faith, each, indeed, claim to embody the true
faith, but each putting it in the special form in which
the particular Church held it; so that we hear no longer
of the doctrine of the Church at large, but of the doctrine
of the Church of Rome, of the Church of England, of the
Church of Geneva, and so forth. So that we seem to
recognize three distinct stages in the history of creeds :
the first, when they express the faith of individuals as
claiming membership in the Church ; the second, when
they express the faith which the Church universal imposes
on individuals ; the third, when they serve to mark what
is distinctive in a particular Church, and are intended to
express what " this Church and realm hath received."

I pointed out in a former lecture that the view which
regarded Scripture as a complete and systematic revelation, of equal authority in all its parts, led naturally to
the use of it as a religious text-book, from which were
drawn the axioms of Christian theology. According
to this view, when the text of Scripture has been
adequately expounded, no farther advance would be
possible in religious knowledge ; all that would remain
would be to defend the faith against attacks. And,
accordingly, we find that each successive statement of

the faith was looked on as final. The Council of Ephesus forbade any addition to the original Nicene symbol.[1] The so-called creed of St. Athanasius declares "Hæc est fides Catholica." The declaration of King James, prefixed to the Thirty-nine Articles, lays down "That if any Divine in the Universities shall preach or print anything either way, other than is already established in Convocation with Our Royal Assent, the Offenders shall be liable to Our displeasure and the Church's censure." And the Welsh Calvinistic Methodists append to their formulary of faith the words, "No alteration in these tenets of Doctrines shall be at any time allowed or even discussed."[2]

And yet, do what we will, no such finality is attainable. Indeed, we cannot without an effort realize under what very various aspects even fundamental doctrines have been regarded at different stages of the Church's life. Take, for example, the doctrine of the relation of the death of Christ to the Christian. Beginning from the simple statement of Christ Himself, that He came to give His life a ransom for many, that the Good Shepherd giveth His life for the sheep, we have the further statement of St. Paul, that we are justified by Christ's Blood ; of St. Peter, that He carried up our sins in His own Body to the tree ; of the Epistle to the Hebrews, that He was once offered to bear the sins

[1] Bishops and clergy framing or propounding any other creed παρὰ τὴν ὁρισθεῖσαν παρὰ τῶν ἁγίων πατέρων were deposed, and laymen anathematized. Cf. Smith's "Dict. of Eccl. Ant.," i. 615 ; Lumby's "Hist. of Creeds," p. 76.

[2] "Constit. Deed," Aug. 10, 1826.

of many.   But men were not content without more precise and formal definition; and the idea of a ransom
was expanded into that of a price paid; but to whom ?
To Satan, was the first answer, by whom we had been
taken captive, and whom Christ beguiled for our deliverance.   To God, was the second answer, Who, by reason
of our debts, had claims upon us which no less price
could discharge.   From this answer arose the theory of
the schoolmen as formulated by Anselm,[1] that man's sin
had robbed God of the honour due to Him; that it was
impossible, God being what He is, that this should
remain so ; that the sinner must make satisfaction to
God, or undergo the penalty of his sin; that Christ,
having made, as He alone could make, a voluntary
offering in His death, had made a full satisfaction for
man's sin.   But beyond this rose the further theory of
Calvinistic Protestantism, that Christ underwent the
accumulated punishment of man's sin, and endured in
his stead the pains of Hell to satisfy the Father's justice ;[2]
a view which we are surprised to find even in Bishop
Heber's hymn—

> " For us He gave His Blood to flow,
>   And met His Father's anger."

---

[1] " Cur Deus Homo," i., c. 13 :   " Nihil minus tolerandum est
in rerum ordine, quam ut creatura creatori debitum honorem
auferat, et non solvat, quod aufert. . . . Necesse est ergo, ut aut
ablatus honor solvatur, aut pœna sequatur."

[2] Gerhard, *loc.* " Theol.," xvii. 2, c. 54. Quoted by Hagenbach,
"Dogmengeschichte."—"Quomodo a maledicto legis nos redemisset,
factus pro nobis maledictum, nisi judicium Dei irati persensisset?"
The Heidelberg Catechism maintains that Christ bore the wrath
of God during all His earthly life.

And if we ask what is the view of the atonement that satisfies the religious instinct of the present day, the reply will probably be that modern religion tends to regard it as the great expression at once of the righteousness and of the love of God.

I have taken this instance of the doctrine of the atonement, because it is clear that in this crucial case of what is usually regarded as the central truth of Christianity, there has been a development, an onward movement in the views of Christian thinkers, and that the view of one age did not adequately meet the needs of another. The theory of the development of Christian doctrine, which came upon the world forty-six years ago with the shock of novelty, and which was then put forward in defence of dogmas which their opponents challenged as being not primitive, has since then been admitted with whatever modifications by almost all who have thought about the matter. In this respect, as in others, we find that God's ways are not our ways. We start with a preconceived notion that truth was revealed once for all in its completeness. But we find that He does not make His truth known to us in a series of propositions, but in a Living Spirit : by that Spirit He teaches the hearts of His people, and leads them on into ever fresh knowledge of Him. And thus we learn that the first requisite for a theologian is to have an open mind ; to be ready to hear God's Voice speaking to him, not in Scripture only, but in the developments of history, in the movements of human thought, in the revelations of science ; to say always, "Speak, Lord, for Thy servant heareth." It is true that there is such a thing as "the faith once for all delivered to the saints;" but it is also true that that faith is not a dead but a living thing, not of the letter, but of the spirit. And, being so, it needs to be spiritually apprehended: it cannot be precipitated into a final and unalterable form, but it must be capable of growth and modification and development. The history of Christian doctrine, a thing hardly conceived of before this century, has now been admitted as an important branch of Church history. And if once we admit that doctrine has a history, it is clear that confessions of faith, which used to be regarded as final expositions of religious truth, are after all to be looked upon rather as historical monuments, marking the level of Christian thought at a given time, than as the moulds by which religious faith is to be shaped in all ages. So far, indeed, as they are simply the statement of the historic basis of the faith, the confession of such belief as justifies a claim to the Christian name, so far as they are but the legitimate expansion of the baptismal formula, so far creeds may be regarded, first as *tesserœ*, or badges of Christian profession, and, secondly, as triumphant hymns of faith; as acts of allegiance to Christ, and as the expression of the unity of all who believe in Him. In this sense, creeds are part of the heritage of the universal Church, witnesses of the unity of Christians, even of those who do not express their belief in the traditional forms. But as soon as a confession of faith is used as a symbol, not of unity, but of division,—as soon as its terms are calculated, not for comprehension, but for exclusion,—it is marked as being of a temporary character; it may express adequately the religious thought of the generation which evolves it, but it is not—it does not profess to be—Catholic, it aims at formulating, not the truth simply, but that aspect of the truth which commends itself to a particular age or nation. Indeed, the further we go back towards Apostolic days, the more do we find that the earliest statements of Christian faith were simply the rehearsal of the elementary facts of which the Apostles were witnesses. What was the παράδοσις—the tradition which St. Paul delivered to the Corinthian Church?— how that Christ died for our sins according to the Scriptures, and that He was buried, and that He rose again according to the Scriptures. Almost equally simple and elementary are the creeds, or rudiments of creeds, which we find in the writings of Irenæus, of Tertullian, of Cyprian. On the other hand, in the *Quincunque vult*, whatever its date and whatever its authorship, we seem to have arrived at the ultimate stage of minute metaphysical definition. So that we may distinguish four successive stages in the development of creeds and formulas of belief: first, the simple statement of belief in God the Father, and in Jesus Christ His only Son, and in the Holy Spirit; then, certain elementary doctrines involved in this belief—the Catholic Church, the remission of sins, the resurrection, and the life everlasting; thirdly, elaborate metaphysical dogmas as to the nature of the Godhead; and finally, inferences as to the relations of God and man, taking shape in the doctrines of predestination, justification, grace, the sacraments, and the like. In the presence of such phenomena, we are obliged to inquire, What is the true object of creeds, and how may that object best be attained?

We must not allow ourselves to forget the original connection of the creed with Baptism. The reply of Philip the Deacon to the Ethiopian Eunuch when he proposed to be baptized at once—" If thou believest with all thy heart thou mayest ;" and the Eunuch's confession —" I believe that Jesus Christ is the Son of God,"—is indeed acknowledged to be an interpolation ; but it expresses exactly the view of the early Church with reference to Baptism. The earliest function of the creed, the only function that it performed in the primitive Church, was to be the expression of the unity of all who professed and called themselves Christians. The use of the plural number—"We believe "—in the Eastern forms of creed, the prohibition to reduce the creed to writing lest it should be communicated to those who were not yet Christians,[1] the restriction of its use to Baptism and the Eucharist, all point to the fact that the

[1] Cf. Aug., Serm. 212: " Nec ut eadem verba symboli teneatis ullo modo debetis scribere, sed audiendo perdiscere, nec cum didiceritis scribere, sed memoria semper tenere atque recolere." He gives as the reason for this prohibition the Divine promise, " I will put My law in their inward parts, and in their heart will I write it." " Hujus rei significandæ causa audiendo symbolum discitur, nec in tabulis, vel in aliqua materia, sed in corde scribitur." But it is probable that the real reason was the fear of profanation. Cyprian applies to the creed the words, " Give not that which is holy to the dogs," etc.

only distinction marked by the creed was the distinction between Christians and those who, whether as Jews or heathen, were outside the Church. Its ground-tone was comprehension, not exclusion. And this is an important point to notice. For it makes a very great difference whether we regard the Catholic Church as a number of individuals who have associated themselves together because they hold the same views on certain matters of theological opinion, or as a great society united together not by identity of opinion but by a living faith in a common Father and in obedience to a common Master. And as soon as confessions of faith are constructed with a view to exclusion and not to comprehension, they at once change their character, and become instruments of closing instead of opening the door of admission to Christian communion. We cannot find a better illustration of this change in the character of confessions of faith than in contrasting the Apostles' and the Nicene Creeds, on the one hand, with the *Quicunque vult* on the other. In the earlier creeds there is but one negative— "Begotten, not made;" in the later there are twenty-one; the object of the former being mainly to affirm positive truth, that of the latter to deny and to anathematize error. And whereas the earlier creeds, with the exception of a few clauses in the Nicene, are confined to historic statements or the simplest deductions from them, the later one revels in the minutest metaphysical distinctions, and seems to aim at arriving by an exhaustive process at a complete definition of God. It does not fall within the subject of this lecture to discuss the question

L

of the position of the so-called Athanasian Creed among the formularies of the English Church, except to remark that as an act of public worship it seems to savour rather of the letter than of the spirit, and that if regarded as a hymn (and an ancient title calls it the Psalm *Quicunque vult* [1]), it is singularly lacking in that element of emotion which is indispensable in a Christian hymn. It is true that the use of creeds in the worship of the Church suggests that they should be regarded rather after the spirit than after the letter; in the words of Dr. Arnold, "Not as reviving the memory of old disputes, and a sort of declaration of war against those who may not agree with us in them, but as principally a free and triumphant expression of thanksgiving to God for all the mighty works which He has done for us." [2] But in the case of the *Quicunque vult* the difficulty is that its letter is, to ordinary worshippers, unintelligible and even misleading, and that its spirit is scarcely that of the meekness and gentleness of Christ. The creed itself is doubtless a valuable monument in the history of theological science, but surely the sober judgment of the mass of devout Christians would agree with the weighty words of Bishop Thirlwall, that "viewed in the light of the fundamental principles of a Reformed Church, it appears, as forming part of our public services, utterly indefensible." [3]

[1] Walter de Cantilupe, Bishop of Worcester, exhorts his clergy, "Habeat etiam saltem quilibet eorum simplicem intellectum, secundum quod continetur in Psalmo qui dicitur, Quicunque vult," etc.

[2] Arnold's "Sermons," vol. iii., p. 276.

[3] See "Report of the Ritual Commission," 1868. Since the Church of Ireland has discontinued the public use of the Athana-

It would seem, then, that creeds should be regarded as symbols of unity, not of division; as instruments of comprehension, not of exclusion. And if we so regard them, questions of detail will become comparatively insignificant. Already time, the universal solvent, has taken off the rough edge of many a subject of controversy. How impossible would it be, for example, to revive any but an antiquarian interest in the great controversy which raged round the *Filioque* clause, and which rent the Church asunder!—and that, not because men care less for the knowledge of God, but because, let us hope, they have come to see that the knowledge of God which is life eternal consists not in the acceptance of logical propositions, but in the inner knowledge which springs from love. How little does the Pelagian controversy touch our religious sentiment, even when it is lighted up by the genius of St. Augustine! Or, to come nearer to our own day, how little can we now enter into or understand the intense eagerness with which thirty-eight years ago the decision in the Gorham case was awaited! And if in our day theological controversy seems to be concentrating itself round the primary article of the creed, the belief in God the Father Almighty, this may at least serve to recall the minds of Christian men to a truer sense of the

sian Creed, the Church of England, with the Episcopal Church of Scotland, stands absolutely alone among Christian Churches in ordering the public use of this formula. It is true that in the Roman Breviary it is ordered to be said at Prime on Sundays; but it is practically unknown to the people, or, if known, only as a form of private devotion.

proportion of things, and to teach them to close their
ranks in preparation for the great issue. In truth, the
whole area of religious thought has changed. The
battle has been fought out on one side of the field,
and has rolled away to quite another, where it has
to be fought, if with the same standards and watchwords, yet with different weapons and under different
conditions.

At such a time it is more than ever necessary to
bear in mind that the Christian faith is not of the letter,
but of the spirit ; not a formula, but a force, an influence,
a life. The promise made by Christ to His disciples
that the Spirit of Truth whom He would send should
lead them into all the truth, was not to them only, but
to those also who should believe on Him through their
word. And it cannot be that in an age like this, when
the knowledge of truth is an object of more eager and
anxious effort than at any time before, His promise
should fail. If indeed we did not believe that the
Spirit of God was still at work, leading men through
darkness into light, through error into truth, through
doubt and perplexity and ignorance into the clear light
and true knowledge of Him, and of His Son Jesus Christ,
we might be alarmed at the outlook. Or if we thought
that the cause of God depended on human institutions
or human formulas, if we did not believe that He is
Immensus, Incomprehensible, not to be measured or
comprehended by our thoughts or definitions of Him,
then we might well tremble lest in the new world which
is before us Man should be all and there should be no

place for God. But even as Christ told His disciples
that it was expedient for them that He should go away,
because if He went not away the Comforter would not
come to them, so it may be He says to us, It is expedient for you that the letter, the outward things in
which you have trusted, and in which you have seemed
to recognize My Presence, should pass away, in order
that the Spirit of Truth may lead you into yet higher
truth and yet clearer knowledge. We need all of us to
learn that our modes of thought are but provisional ;
that forms of doctrine and of worship need to be
quickened by the ever-fresh life of the Spirit ; that " it
is the Spirit that quickeneth, the flesh profiteth nothing;"
that, in the pregnant words of Edward Irving, " When
the Holy Ghost departs from any set of opinions or
form of character, they wither like a sapless tree."[1]

But, it may be said, the Catholic faith surely is
unchanged and unchangeable ? It is unchanged, just as
the tree is unchanged which has put forth the vital
energy which makes it what it is, and has grown from
a young sapling into a stately oak. It is unchangeable,
and yet we are sure that as the ages roll by, and as social
conditions change and " the thoughts of men are
widened with the progress of the suns," it will assume
fresh proportions, and will put forth fresh shoots, and
will imperceptibly adapt itself to its environment. Of
all heresies the greatest and the most deadly is that
which would limit God's revelation of Himself to one
age or to one type of character or to one system of

---

[1] Life of Edward Irving, i., p. 347.

thought. In Christ are all the treasures of wisdom and knowledge hidden. They are hidden that we may search them out, that we may expect ever fresh light and fresh knowledge to break forth from Him. " I am verily persuaded," said the Pastor of the Pilgrim Fathers as they embarked in the *Mayflower*[1] —" I am verily persuaded that the Lord has more truth yet to break forth out of His word." "It is not incredible," says Bishop Butler,[2] " that a book which has been so long in the possession of mankind should contain many truths as yet undiscovered." "O send forth Thy light and Thy truth that they may lead me," should be the prayer, as of each Christian man, so too of the Church at large. "Lord, to whom shall we go ? Thou hast the words of eternal life."

It is a very natural mistake to suppose that because Christianity is perfect, therefore there can be no growth or progress in it. But it is more true to say that its very perfection implies growth. As Cardinal Newman says,[3] " Here below to live is to change ; and to be perfect is to have changed often ; " and again, " In such an idea as Christianity, developments cannot but be, and these surely Divine, because it is Divine." It is true that the author of the " Development of Christian Doctrine " was forging a weapon to be used in defence of the Church of his adoption, and that he would repudiate all development but such as proceeds on certain definite

---

[1] Quoted by J. M. Wilson, " Essays," p. 110.
[2] " Analogy," pt. ii., c. 3.
[3] Essay on " Development," p. 40.

lines of Church authority; but such weapons have a double edge, and if once the principle of the development of doctrine is admitted, it is difficult and hardly reverent to prescribe beforehand in what direction the Spirit shall lead men's minds. "Securus judicat orbis terrarum," is a motto which may be susceptible, in these later days, of a wider meaning than was assigned to it either by St. Augustine or by Cardinal Newman.

There is a touching passage, such as he alone could have written, in the last-named author's book on "Development,"—a book written after he had withdrawn to Littlemore, when he was preparing himself to face the separation which he had now recognized as inevitable,—on which we in modern Oxford may do well to ponder. Arguing that "the Roman Catholic communion of this day is the successor and representative of the mediæval Church," and "that the mediæval Church is the legitimate heir of the Nicene," he says, "Did St. Athanasius or St. Ambrose suddenly come to life, it cannot be doubted what communion he would mistake for his own. All surely will agree that these Fathers, with whatever opinions of their own, whatever protests, if we will, would find themselves more at home with such men as St. Bernard or St. Ignatius Loyola, or with the lonely priest in his lodging, or the holy sisterhood of mercy, or the unlettered crowd before the altar, than with the teachers or with the members of any other creed. And may we not add, that were those same Saints, who once sojourned, one in exile and one in embassy, at Treves, to come more northward still, and to travel until they reached another fair city, seated among groves, green meadows, and calm streams, the holy brothers would turn from many a high aisle and solemn cloister which they found there, and ask the way to some small chapel where mass was said in the populous alley or forlorn suburb ? " It would be obvious to retort with the question, " If St. Paul could come to life, where would *he* find himself most at home ? " But, passing by this, I think that there is a fallacy lurking somewhere in this passage, and that we may find it in the little word *suddenly*. No doubt if a Saint of the early Church should suddenly come to life, knowing nothing of all the history of thought and of science and of social life in the interval, he might well be perplexed by what he would find, and he might very possibly find what he sought in "some small chapel in a forlorn suburb." But what is this but an admission that the small chapel in a forlorn suburb has kept itself aloof from the main current of Church life, and that Christian thought has swept by and has left it forlorn ? It is the same fallacy that met us in University Reform. When it was proposed to throw open the foundations and reform the colleges, it was asked, " What would the great mediæval founders, Wykeham and Waynflete, if they could suddenly come to life, say to the proposal to alter the conditions of their foundations ? " The reply was obvious, that if those great men had lived continuously from the fourteenth and fifteenth to the nineteenth century, they would undoubtedly have moved with the age, and would have been the first to acknowledge that the letter must give way to the spirit, and that the identity of a living and growing body is truer than that of a cold and dead and unchanging statue. And in the same way, if St. Athanasius and St. Ambrose had lived through the decline and fall of the Empire, through the Middle Ages, through the revival of learning, through the Reformation, through the growth of the modern world out of feudalism, can we believe that they would have stood still? Is it conceivable that the greatest and best men of the fourth century would have rejected and disowned all the developments of modern life and modern society and modern thought? Surely no more than they would have refused to avail themselves of modern speech, and modern dress, and modern sanitary laws, and modern means of communication. It is we, not they, who are the ancients; we who possess accumulated stores of experience; we who can see things in truer proportion, and interpret more justly the ways of God to man. To tie modern life to the forms of ancient thought and ancient worship is surely a Mezentian cruelty.

What, then, should be our attitude in relation to creeds and confessions of faith? Are we to regard them simply as historical monuments, records of past phases of religious thought, witnesses of the belief of the age which gave them birth; or are they more than this? Probably the truest estimate we can form of them is to regard them in connexion with worship, as expressions of the Church's triumphant faith addressed to God. Indeed, the highest type of creed may be found in the

Te Deum, that great hymn of mingled thanksgiving and prayer and faith.   And if we adhere to this view, we shall see how wide is the difference in character between the ancient Baptismal and Eucharistic Creeds on the one hand, and on the other the more modern confessions, as the decrees of the Council of Trent, the Thirty-nine Articles, the Confession of Augsburg, or the Westminster Confession.   If, indeed, we require rigid and minute tests of orthodoxy, it is better that for such a purpose we should use modern forms ; the ancient Catholic creeds should be kept sacred from controversial use.   For, in truth, we are taking a perverted view of the Christian Covenant if we make Christian unity consist in agreement in abstract doctrine.   It has been well said [1] that " the Christian Church is a body of worshippers and not of philosophers ; a body of men whose relations to each other are constituted by their common relation to a mysterious Person in Whom they believe, as a Mediator between them and God. . . . The faith required of a man to be a Christian is faith in a Person and not in a system ; faith in facts and promises more than in dogmas or in truths."   Surely if ecclesiastical history teaches us anything, it is this, that the attempt to mould men's thoughts into a single type is destined to failure.   The unity of the Christian Church is to be sought, not primarily in uniformity of organization, nor in identity of theological dogma, but in the unity of the spirit, in the bond of peace.   Let us seek and pray for that, the

[1] Myers, "Catholic Thoughts on the Church of Christ and the Church of England," p. 119.

only true unity; let us follow after things that make for peace, and things whereby one may edify another; let us learn to love one another, and to understand one another, and to respect one another, and to help one another; let us recite the creeds as expressions of trust in our Father's love, of loyalty to Christ our Master, of unity in the life of the Spirit; and for the rest, let us leave it in God's hand to work out in His way and in His time an answer to the prayer of Christ, which assuredly cannot fail, "That they all may be one; as Thou, Father, art in Me, and I in Thee, that they also may be in Us; that the world may believe that Thou didst send Me."

LECTURE VII.

IN CHRISTIAN WORSHIP AND LIFE.

"We serve in newness of the spirit, and not in oldness of the letter."—Rom. vii. 6.

In the last two lectures we discussed the letter and the spirit in relation to the Sacraments and Creeds of the Church, and we seemed to recognize in each of them a permanent element, an element not of separation but of unity, not of exclusion but of comprehension. We turn to-day to the more general subject of Christian worship and the Christian life.

As soon as our minds become conscious of the idea of a Power above ourselves, the question arises, Do we stand in any kind of relation to that Power? And if the Power takes in our thoughts the form of a Being whose favour or displeasure can affect our happiness or well-being, it becomes an important question, How can we propitiate Him? And since our tendency is to think that God is even such an one as ourselves, we are inclined to regard Him as we should wish our inferiors to regard us. The speculations of Caliban in Browning's poem represent too many of men's thoughts about God.[1]

[1] Browning, "Caliban upon Setebos."

" He is strong and Lord.
'Am strong myself compared to yonder crabs
That march now from the mountain to the sea :
'Let twenty pass, and stone the twenty-first,
Loving not, hating not, just choosing so.
As it likes me each time, thus I do : so He."

But when men thus think of God, their worship is the
cringing, grovelling homage of slaves anxious to propitiate a capricious master. They think, " What can I
give to God that He will be pleased with ? What
should I like, if I were God ? I should like something
that I could enjoy, or else some abject acknowledgment
of my power." And so they offer to God meat and drink,
or costly ornaments, or else a life, the life of an animal,
or even of their own child, as representing that life
which they wish to preserve for themselves. But when
God reveals to them a higher conception of Himself, and
they learn that He is a righteous God, they begin to
comprehend that He will not be pleased with thousands
of rams, or with ten thousands of rivers of oil ; that the
sacrifice He requires is a right life, to do justly, and to
love mercy, and to walk humbly with God. And yet
there is a third and still higher revelation of God, when
men know Him not only as Almighty, not only as a
a righteous Judge, but as a loving Father. And then
they know that what He asks of them is, " My son, give
Me thine heart ; " and that the first and great commandment is, " Thou shalt love the Lord thy God with all
thy heart, and with all thy soul, and with all thy mind,
and with all thy strength."

There are, then, three grades of worship, corresponding

to these three grades of knowledge; the worship of
giving or sacrifice, the worship of a right life, and the
worship of a loving and filial heart. And the two
former are not done away, but are included and fulfilled
in the latter. On the great law of love hang all the
Law and the Prophets. It is on this ideal that any
discussion on Christian worship must be based—that
God is not worshipped with men's hands, as though He
needed anything; but that He desires men to offer
themselves to Him from love to their Father in Heaven.
Any worship which starts from a lower ideal than this,
any worship which is not the expression of filial trust
and reverence and love, may be true and genuine, but
is not in the highest sense Christian worship.

It may perhaps help us to arrive at a truer idea of
religious worship, if I recall what I said in my last
lecture as to the meaning of religion. We then saw
that, whereas the popular idea of religion is, that it
consists in certain opinions which a man holds, and
which constitutes a bond of union with those whom he
calls his co-religionists, while they separate him from a
far larger number of those who do not hold the same
doctrines, the root-idea of religion is the yearning of the
spirit of man after the Spirit of God. It matters little
whether we connect the word "religio" etymologically
with "religare," to bind together, or with "relegere," to
ponder, to meditate;[1] the main point is, that religion in
its primary and highest signification is that which the
Psalmist expresses when he cries, "My soul is athirst for

---

[1] Cf. Max Müller's "Lectures on the Science of Religion."

God, yea even for the Living God ; when shall I come to
appear before the Presence of God ? " It is what St.
Augustine expresses in the well-known words—which
who will dare to call uninspired ?—" Thou madest us
for Thyself, and our heart is restless until it rest in
Thee." [1] So far it is undoubtedly true, that the first
stirrings of the religious instinct in the soul have the
effect of " making a man rest in the thought of two, and
two only, supreme and luminously self-evident beings,
himself and his Creator." [2] So far it is true that—to use
a shallow axiom of modern individualism—religion is a
thing between a man's self and his God. But if it does
not go further than this—if it does not teach him that
God's purpose for good is not for himself only but for all
men—if it does not stir in him something of our Lord's
desire " that they all may be one," it is not yet the
religion of Christ. And in the same way, no doubt
worship in the first instance is the uttering of the soul's
trust and love towards God, the entering into the closet
and praying to the Father which is in secret : but it
must go further than this, if it is to carry out the
Christian ideal ; it must be the expression, not of individuality, but of corporate unity ; it must bind together
men of all communions, of all confessions, of all lands,
and of all ages in one communion and fellowship. It is
this that constitutes the great advantage of ancient over
modern forms of devotion. When we use such forms, for
example, as the *Gloria in excelsis,* or the *Sursum corda,*

---

[1] Aug., " Confess.," I., c. i.
[2] Newman's " Apologia."

which we find quoted familiarly, just as we should quote
them ourselves, by writers of the fourth century, do we
not feel that there is in them an elevation, a Catholicity,
which we miss in even the best of modern devotions?
When we sing the *Veni Creator Spiritus*, are we not
conscious of breathing a higher and purer atmosphere
than that of the modern sentimental ditties which are
dignified by the name of hymns? And so with the
ancient Collects : it is not merely that they are redolent
of a simpler, less controversial type of religion ; but also
the mere fact of their having served as the expression
of all that was highest and noblest in a succession of
Christian generations gives them a universal currency
which cannot attach to the coinage of a more recent
religious mint. No doubt, the mediæval Church had
reduced religious worship to a service of the letter, an
unspiritual *battologia*, which needed a reaction ; and we
can hardly wonder that men, awakening to the consciousness of the awfulness of the communion of the soul
with God, should have thought that the only way of
vindicating the supremacy of the spirit was to cast off
the letter altogether, and that worship to be true and
genuine must be the simple spontaneous expression of
the religious consciousness of the moment. But still,
those Christian communities suffered grievous loss which
in the fervour of the Reformation cut themselves off
from the ancient liturgies. One rejoices to see symptoms
that they are becoming conscious of the loss, and that
they are beginning to claim their share in the rich devotional heritage which the ancient Church has bequeathed

to us. For this reason, one cannot without regret hear
the Book of Common Prayer spoken of as though it
were the exclusive and distinctive property of a single
religious community ; and one rejoices in the declaration
of a late chairman of the Congregational Union,[1] that all
the twelve tribes of Israel claim their part in the English
Prayer-Book. As with the Sacraments and the creeds,
so with all other devotional forms ; the more we can
regard them as setting forth the unity of Christians,
and the less we think of them as badges of separation,
the better it will be for ourselves and for the Church at
large. Surely if Christians would nourish their spiritual
life mainly on the simple but solid food of the ancient
forms of worship, while at the same time they threw
themselves without reserve or scruple into the swing of
modern life, they would be approaching more nearly to
the ideal, not of a primitive Christian, nor yet of a
nineteenth century Christian, but of a Catholic Christian,
and, praying in the spirit, they might be more anxious
to keep the unity of the spirit in the bond of peace. It
is no small gain to use in our common worship forms
which are for the most part older than any of our
existing divisions.

And yet we must always remember that it is not in
forms, nor yet in the absence of forms, that any security
can be found for spiritual worship. "God is a Spirit ; and
they that worship Him must worship Him in spirit and
in truth"—this is the fundamental rubric on which all
depends. One cannot but fear lest the revived interest

[1] Rev. E. White.

M

in ritual which has grown out of the Oxford movement,
attractive and helpful as much of it may be, should
tend to make religion a matter of what Carlyle calls
"rhythmic drill," a matter of attendance at Holy Communion, of observance of rules, of membership of guilds
and the like; and lest, in the stress laid upon the outward,
the inward should be lost sight of. Among young men
especially, there is great fear lest the over-systematizing
of religion, the tendency to reduce it to a mechanical
uniformity, should destroy that individuality, that
spontaneousness, which gives to personal religion its true
value. I admit that for all except perhaps the strongest
types of character some kind of outward framework,
some system and method in the religious life, is a useful
and even necessary help; but let us never forget that
throughout the New Testament variety and not uniformity is set forth as the characteristic result of the
working of the Spirit of God. Whatever forms we may
find useful to ourselves, let us use them, provided we do
not suffer them to obscure the end to which they are
but means : but let us bear in mind two things; first,
that forms need to be continually kept living and fresh
by the quickening Spirit, and that without this they
will become lifeless and corrupt; and secondly, that we
must not set up our own practice as the standard for
others, for that St. Paul's caution applies to this subject
—" Who art thou that judgest the servant of another ?
to his own lord he standeth or falleth." The kingdom
of God is not in word — not in profession, not in
observances—but in power; in victory over evil, in a

life of Christian activity. *Laborare est orare* is a motto
which is capable of being pushed to a dangerous extreme,
and outward activity is of the letter that killeth unless
it be stirred and regulated by the spirit of power and
love and discipline ; but we shall do harm to the cause
of Christian boldness if we allow the idea of religion to
be associated rather with the θρησκεία of observances
than with that of active usefulness.

But to return to worship in the more abstract sense,
it may be useful to ask, What is it that marks it as
distinctively Christian ? We may, of course, assume that
it must be spiritual, or, in other words, that it must be
not outward and mechanical merely, but the expression
of the devotion of the heart ; but further than this, to
make it Christian, it must be offered in the Name of
Christ : "Whatsoever ye shall ask of the Father in My
Name, He will give it you." It has generally been held
that prayer in the Name of Christ implied the invocation
of His Name or of His merits ; and so it has been
customary in the Western Church to conclude all prayers
addressed to the Father with the Name of Jesus Christ.
It is well that we should do so, if only to associate our
worship expressly with Him through Whom we have our
access in one Spirit unto the Father : but we must not
think that the mere naming of His Name is all that is
required, we must not treat the Name of Christ as a
kind of charm by which to commend our prayers to
God ; rather, as we were baptized into Jesus Christ, as
He is the element wherein the whole Christian life
moves, as whatsoever we do, in word or deed, we are to

do all in the Name of the Lord Jesus, so prayer above all, which is the expressing and the presenting to God of the whole life, must be done in conscious connexion with Christ, must be offered by us as being one with Him. As Luthardt well expresses it, he prays in Christ's Name who is in Christ.[1] The essence of prayer is, that it should be offered in a filial spirit; and all such prayer is offered to the Father in the Son's Name, whether or not the Name of Christ is spoken. He who says from his heart "Our Father," prays in Christ's Name. To pray in the Name of Jesus Christ is to pray as He prayed, " Father, not my will, but Thine be done."

And from this it would appear that Theism, which professes to accept Christ as a Teacher and an Example but not as a Mediator, is in fact, not an advance to a more spiritual conception of religion, but rather a falling back under the dominion of the letter. For Christ came not to proclaim only, but to carry into effect the will of the Father, through Him to reconcile all things unto Himself—and if men are able to cry " Abba, Father," it is through the Spirit of Christ in their hearts, even

[1] Luthardt, " Johann. Evang.," ii., p. 306: " Im Namen Christi betet, wer, indem er betet, ἐν Χριστῷ ist und als ἐν Χριστῷ seiender zu Gott betet." And *cf.* Campbell, " The Bread of Life," p. 96: " The law of the kingdom of God, according to which prayer in the Name of the Son is answered, and that according to which prayer for things according to the Father's Will is answered, are one and the same law. For to ask in the Name of the Son, is to ask in the light of His Name in Whom the Father is well pleased. In answering such prayer, God is not granting for Christ's sake what for His Own sake He would not grant. He is granting that which His delight in Christ reveals His eternal willingness to grant."

though they may think that they are coming to the
Father independently of Him. No man cometh unto
the Father but by Him; and if men feel in their hearts
a yearning after God, if they feel a craving which
nothing but God can satisfy, we may confidently leave
them in the hand of the Good Shepherd, and trust that
He will carry out in them His perfect work, and lead
them in the way everlasting. There is indeed some truth
in Pascal's remark, that the knowledge of God, without
Jesus Christ, is useless and barren.[1] For any conception
of God which professes to be independent of Christ is
either derived from the Christian tradition, or else is a
more or less dreary denial of the possibility of any true
spiritual communion with God, a religion of timid and
tentative affirmations, and of bold and dogmatic nega-
tions. It is a delusion to imagine that a pure Theism is
a more spiritual form of belief than Christianity. More
spiritual it may be than the traditional Christianity
which consists in rigid and stereotyped forms of practice,
of ceremonial, of observance, of dogma; but not more
spiritual than the teaching of Christ Himself, the end
and completion of Whose work was to bring men to the
Father, to teach them that God is a Spirit, and to send
the Spirit of the Father into the hearts of His disciples.
It would be a strange perversity if men should reject
Christ in the name of spiritual religion, when it is to
Christ and to Him alone that they owe the conception
of what spiritual religion is.

The acceptance of the spiritual rather than the

---

[1] Pascal, "Pensées," xiv. 2.

literal view of worship would have acted as a solvent in
many controversies. Take, for example, the question of
prayers for the departed. That it was the custom of
the Church from the earliest times to pray for the dead
is beyond all question.[1] Tertullian, Origen, St. Chrysostom, St. Augustine, and, indeed, all early writers
assume it as the established practice. In truth, the
vivid sense which the early Church possessed of the
communion of Saints, the belief that the dead, like
the living, are in Christ, that all live unto God, made
it impossible for them to pray for the one without the
other. But men were not content to observe this as
a pious and beautiful practice ; they asked, " In what are
the dead benefited by our prayers ? " And so there sprang
up the theory that by the prayers of the living the
purgatorial sufferings of the dead were mitigated and
shortened ; and then came masses for the dead, alms to
help souls out of purgatory, and all the lucrative traffic
of the mediæval Church. This is not the only natural
and harmless practice that has been turned by the
interest of the priesthood and the credulity of the people
into a gross and carnal superstition. And so at the
Reformation it was inevitable that the whole thing should
be swept away, and that logic should prevail over feeling, and that prayers for the departed should disappear
from the service-books of the Church. And yet, does
not a human instinct sometimes rebel against the stern
logic of Protestantism ? Does not a parent who has lost
a child sometimes refuse to banish the loved and familiar

[1] See authorities in Bingham, "Antiq.," xv. iii. § 16.

name from his prayers, simply because the child who
bears it has gone home to his Father in Heaven? If,
indeed, we are to apply to prayer the inexorable test of
results, there may be many a prayer that we shall hardly
dare to offer ; but if we pray because we know that God
our Father would have us open our hearts to Him, and
because we believe that those whom we love are in His
hands, then no dogma and no fear of superstition need
hinder us from asking Him to bless them, and to let the
light of His countenance shine upon them and His
perpetual Presence comfort them.

I have already, in a former lecture, pointed out how
largely the letter has prevailed over the spirit in the
Sacraments, especially in the Eucharist. But in connexion with this latter act of worship, it may be well to
touch upon one or two incidental points, on which the
principle for which I am contending has an important
bearing. Great stress is now being laid by a section of
the clergy of the Church of England on the practice
of fasting communion. Young persons are urged always
to communicate at early celebrations, and communion
otherwise than fasting is regarded as a profanation of
the Holy Mysteries. It is enforced, not on the rational
ground that fasting tends to keep the mind clear and is
a means of subduing the flesh, but on purely physical
and materialistic grounds. " Remember "—so says a
little book on the ceremonial of the Altar,[1] drawn up for

---

[1] " The Ceremonial of the Altar." Compiled by a Priest. Swan
Sonnenschein and Co. The aim of this book is " to put the student
in possession of the traditions on the method of saying Mass, which

the use of loyal sons of the Church of England—"Remember that the fast from midnight before Communion is rigorous, and that a lozenge or a sip of water breaks it as effectually as the heaviest meal." It is difficult to speak with patience of such a caricature of the religion of Christ. It is difficult to conceive that the teachers of such a system can ascribe any authority to the words of Christ, "The flesh profiteth nothing," or to those of St. Paul, "The kingdom of God is not meat and drink." At least one may be allowed to describe such teaching in the words of Bishop Wilberforce,[1] spoken in his last

the compilers of our Prayer-Book presupposed to exist." The following is a sample: "As you give out the Gospel, place the left hand on the book, and with the right thumb make a small sign of the Cross on the book at the commencement of the Gospel you are about to read. Then, at once transferring the left hand to the breast, make similar signs with the right thumb on your forehead and on your breast. The fingers meanwhile are extended, and the palms are turned inwards."

There are full directions as to the ceremonial to be observed when the Blessed Sacrament is exposed for adoration, or placed veiled on the Altar.

The perusal of this book is likely to be instructive to "loyal sons of the Church of England."

[1] The quotation is from "an Address delivered by the late Bishop of Winchester to the Rural Deans of the Diocese at Winchester House, July 15, 1873." The Report was printed shortly after his death, which took place on July 19th, and was "carefully prepared by comparison of notes taken at the time." He says, "It is difficult to estimate the mischief which is resulting from the action of the High Ritualistic party in this matter. . . It is not in a light sense that I say this new doctrine of Fasting Communion is dangerous. The practice is not advocated because a man comes in a clearer spirit and less disturbed body and mind, able to give himself entirely to prayer and communion with his God; but on a miserable degraded notion that the consecrated elements will meet with other food in the stomach. It is a detestable materialism."

public utterance before his death : " It is a detestable materialism."

Closely connected with this is the subject of evening celebrations of the Holy Communion. This is a question which was fully dealt with in the notes to Dr. Hessey's well-known Bampton Lectures on the subject of Sunday, but which may be touched upon briefly as illustrating our present subject. With many of the objections urged against this modern practice it is possible to feel much sympathy. There is much in the general though not universal practice of the Church from primitive times to the nineteenth century ; there is much in the preference of the earlier and more tranquil hours of the day for the solemnities of religion ; there is much in the fear lest persons should come to evening Communions in a state either of lassitude or of excitement. But still, if it is true that there are large classes of persons who are absolutely unable to attend in the earlier hours of the day, it is surely competent for every particular or national Church,[1] having " authority to ordain, change, and abolish, ceremonies or rites of the Church ordained only by man's authority " (and it is impossible to contend that Christ ordained early celebrations when He instituted His Supper in the evening)—it is, I say, surely competent for a Church or even for a particular congregation to revert to the earliest use, and to celebrate the Eucharist in the evening. For, as I tried to point out in an earlier lecture, the essence of the Eucharist lies, not in the mere ceremonial observance, but in the spirit of devotion to

[1] Article XXXIV.

Christ, and of hopeful looking for His kingdom, and of brotherly helpfulness to our fellow-men ; and these things depend not on the hour of celebration, but on the attitude of the heart towards God.   The great principle which our Lord laid down, " The Sabbath was made for man, and not man for the Sabbath," is conclusive as to all matters of mere outward regulation and order ; it tells us that the well-being, the edification, even the convenience of man is superior to all observance of the letter for its own sake ; and that if we exalt ceremonial regulations into Divine laws we are trenching on the authority of the Son of Man, who is Lord, as of the sabbath, so also of all else that affects the welfare of His people.   One cannot but fear that, in the scrupulous attention which is paid to matters of this kind in the present day, there is something of timidity lest by asserting our Christian liberty we should be widening the breach between ourselves and the Church of Rome.   But surely we of the Church of England are strong enough to take our own ground in these matters ; and assuredly no amount of conformity to so-called Catholic usage, short of absolute surrender to the Papal authority, will win for us any kind of recognition from the Roman Church.   " With freedom did Christ set us free ; stand fast therefore, and be not entangled again in a yoke of bondage" is an admonition not less needed by us than it was by the Churches of Galatia to whom it was addressed.

The conflict between the letter and the spirit has not been confined to the interpretation of Scripture or to the ecclesiastical sphere : it meets us also in the common

life of Christians. To one who honestly and heartily
desires to live a godly life, it is a question of no small
importance and interest, " How shall I guide my steps ?
What is the authority to which I can turn in all those
many cases of doubt and difficulty which are sure from
time to time to occur ? " To this question various
answers have been given. In one age of the Church,
the reply would have been, " Place your conscience in
the hands of your Confessor. He is divinely autho-
rized to relieve you of all responsibility." At another
time, or by other teachers, the answer would have been
given, " A thorough knowledge of Scripture is the only
means of keeping your life right. Whenever a difficulty emerges, you should have a text ready ; if only
you are accustomed to keep scriptural weapons ready
to hand, the right text will never fail you at the right
moment." And there is yet another answer, to the
effect that moral action, like all other action, depends
on the right application of certain fundamental principles, and that this application must be made, not at
haphazard, but in accordance with definite rules ; and
hence it follows that the study of casuistry, or the
method of ascertaining in each case what is the right
course to follow, is, if not indispensable for ordinary
persons, yet at least a great help for those who would
walk accurately and carefully, and a necessity for those
who are to be moral or religious guides. Yet here, too,
we shall find that the letter killeth ; the man who walks
by a system, the man who has a text or a precedent
always ready, the man who gives his conscience no free

play, but who trusts to being able to refer every difficult question to some rule, as though it were a question
of grammar or mathematics, will become dependent on
his system, and will lose that delicate moral instinct,
that quick perception of right and wrong, which belongs
to those who trust to the guidance of the Spirit of God,
who by reason of use have their senses exercised to
discern good and evil.   Just as in art originality is a
higher and a nobler thing than servile imitation, so in
morals it is better that a man should simply follow his
conscience than that he should act by the advice even
of the wisest confessor or in obedience to even the most
admirable rules.   There is a moral intuition, an instinct
of right and wrong, which is better than all the rules
and all the systems in the world.   The proverb,
" Second thoughts are best," is true of matters of
worldly management and prudence ; it is not true in
questions of morals.   As Bishop Butler says,[1] " In all
common ordinary cases, we see intuitively at first view
what is our duty, what is the honest part.   This is the
ground of the observation, that the first thought is
often the best.   In these cases doubt and deliberation is
itself dishonesty."   " In matters of duty," says Cardinal Newman,   " first thoughts are commonly best—
they have more in them of the voice of God."[2] Or, as
the same distinction is expressed by a modern writer,[3]
" When we consider human action, whether theoretically

[1] Butler's Sermon on Balaam, " Works," ii., p. 84.
[2] Newman's " Sermons," bk. iv., p. 36.
[3] Cf. " Natural Religion," pp. 173–174.

or historically, we are always brought to this fundamental antithesis. Human action is either mechanical
or intelligent, either conventional or rational,—either it
follows custom or reason, either it is guided by rules or
by inspiration. In morals as in poetry, you must be
of the school either of Boileau or of Shakespeare.
Either you must sedulously observe a number of regulations you do not hope to understand, or you must
move freely towards an end you passionately conceive,
at times making new rules for yourself, at times reject-
ing old ones, and allowing to convention only a kind of
provisional or prescriptive validity." And in the formation of the Christian character, the cultivation of this
faculty of trusting to inspiration is of the utmost importance. For what God requires of us is, not right
action simply, but right action as the outcome and
evidence of a right state of the moral being. Here
again we meet with the fundamental distinction between
faith and works. To do right—that is salvation by
works ; to be right—that is salvation by faith.

Upon this same antithesis are based two opposite
theories of government and two opposite systems of
education. In politics, the one tendency is to develop
individuality as far as is consistent with the safety of
the society ; the other, to subordinate the individual to
the society. It is not only in a despotic form of government that individualism is liable to be crushed out ;
democracy is often a still worse tyrant, and enforces its
ideal mediocrity under still heavier penalties. It is one
great danger of modern society, that men born to lead

must so often make choice between being set aside as unpractical, and consenting to follow and not to lead the multitude.

The same opposite tendencies meet us in education.[1] The one system aims at reducing the individual into conformity with a certain type ; to make him a good citizen or a good churchman, or whatever the type may be. Of this, one could hardly find a better example than in the Republic of Plato. To him it appeared that a thorough reform of education was needed as a remedy for the evils of the time. And this reform was to consist in producing conformity in the citizen, according to his capacity and his calling, to an objective type, existing outside of man, in relation to which all his faculties and his tastes were to be trained and moulded. The tendency of modern times, speaking generally, has been to a different system ; to develop freely whatever was in a man, so as to produce, not conformity to a type, but the perfection of the individual. This certainly, with whatever shortcomings, has been the aim of modern university education ; to produce " a succession of persons duly qualified to serve God in Church and State," not by a mechanical process of putting into them certain opinions and certain habits, but by the more spiritual method of educating and developing whatever faculties, whatever possibilities, were implanted in them by God. This must be our reply to those who lament that Oxford is no longer, in the same exclusive sense as she once was,

[1] Some thoughts in this passage were suggested by Mark Pattison's sermon on the subject of " Education."

a nursing mother of the Church of England ; that it is better to take men as they are, and to make what you can of them, than by attempting to impress upon all a special ecclesiastical type to discourage all development except in one direction. We may well trust that the modern system will produce men of various types, capable and desirous of understanding each other's point of view, willing to learn of each other, and each ready to admit that different aspects of the truth may commend themselves to different persons. And if it is asserted that the Universities, admitting as they do without restriction persons of every variety of religious and non-religious belief, are no longer fit places for the training of the clergy of the National Church, we may reply that an atmosphere of liberty, in which all opinions are alike represented and all alike claim to be respected, is a far healthier and more bracing one than that of a theological seminary, in which a man comes into contact with men of only one type, and in which he forms his idea of other systems of religious thought only from the account given of them by their adversaries. If the Church of England is to preserve and extend her claim to the title of the National Church, it can only be by her clergy learning to understand men of other religious systems, and acknowledging that no one body of Christian people can claim a monopoly either of truth or of holiness.

It is far less difficult to give ourselves up to the guidance of a system or of a director than to accept the responsibility of walking by the Spirit. The temptation comes to us in the plausible form of humility and self-distrust. " Surely we are more likely to arrive at truth by taking what Aristotle calls the unproven assertions of the wise, than by painfully hammering out a system for ourselves out of the results of our own thought and experience." It may be so, and we may very reasonably avail ourselves of the labours of others and of the accumulated wisdom of the past ; but still we cannot divest ourselves of our personal responsibility, we cannot adopt the opinions or the rules of other men at second-hand, any more than we can wear their clothes ; for our minds and spirits differ as much as do our bodies, and what fits one man is too wide or too narrow for another. " Where the Spirit of the Lord is, there is liberty." We cannot be children in understanding ; we must walk as men. It is for this reason that one mistrusts the tendency, which appears over and over again in the most various forms, to reduce the Christian life to a system, to rely upon rules rather than upon principles, to fall back upon the oldness of the letter. A striking instance of this is the astonishing way in which, notwithstanding the plain words of St. Paul, Christian people have insisted upon identifying the Lord's Day with the Jewish Sabbath, and have invented a traditional code of Sunday observance which forces upon one's mind the Apostle's words, " I am afraid of you, lest by any means I have bestowed upon you labour in vain." And now the reaction seems to be upon us, and people seem bent upon asserting a liberty which it is difficult to call Christian. It is of little use solemnly to discuss the question, What recreations, if any, are lawful on Sunday? Surely we cannot hesitate to reply, "All things are lawful for me." Yes, but let us not omit the balancing consideration, "But all things are not expedient." It is a matter in which it is more easy but less necessary to assert our Christian liberty than to be careful of the claims of Christian charity. It is better to deny ourselves than, by claiming our full liberty, to hurt the consciences or to abridge the liberty of others.

Another curious instance of the way in which men cling to the letter, to some kind of positive rule, is the assertion which one sometimes hears that God claims at least a tenth of every one's income as an offering to Him. One would have thought that the only Christian principle is, "Whosoever he be of you that forsaketh not all that he hath, he cannot be My disciple." One would have thought that the fixing of a certain definite proportion savours of St. Peter's question, "Lord, how oft shall my brother sin against me, and I forgive him? Until seven times?" Thus Irenæus [1] says that our Lord came to expand and extend the Law, and, instead of definite commands, to substitute principles; and "therefore, instead of, 'Thou shalt not commit adultery,' He commanded men not to lust; and instead of, 'Thou shalt not kill,' not even to be angry; and instead of paying tithe, to divide all one's goods to the poor." Indeed, it is obvious that this rule would be quite inadequate as a moral standard, and that to give a tenth of his income would be to one man no perceptible sacri-

---

[1] Irenæus, "Hær.," iv. 27.

fice at all; while to another, or to the same man at
another period of his life, it would involve the cur-
tailing of his children's education and the neglect to
make provision for his family.   All such hard and fast
rules tend to kill the spontaneousness of Christian beneficence, and to turn it into a matter of calculation.   The
only Christian law is the law of love, and love—

> " Rejects the lore
> Of nicely calculated less or more." [1]

And so we are brought back to the great fundamental principle, which underlies all religion and all
worship, that " Love is the fulfilling of the law ; " that
the only sacrifice that God desires is the sacrifice of a
loving heart ; that if we bestow all our goods to feed
the poor, and if we give our bodies to be burned, and
have not love, it profiteth us nothing.   Prayer, almsgiving, outward observances, all must have their root in
love, or they will become cold and dead and meaningless.   And yet, on the other hand, we may not let our
religion evaporate into a sentiment, a perfume ; we
must serve God not in oldness of the letter, not as a
matter of routine, of law, of respectability, of social
position, but in newness of the spirit, with the new
energy, the new enthusiasm, the new hope, with which
Christ inspires His servants.   Not less but more obedience, not less but more self-sacrifice, is demanded of
those who are not under the Law but under grace.

And if we of the nineteenth century, we upon whom
the ends of the world are come, are ever tempted to

[1] Wordsworth, " Ecclesiastical Sonnets," xliii.

think that we are wiser, more enlightened, more free
from superstitions than men of past generations, and to
despise the simple faith of earlier days, let us see to it
that with our wider knowledge, our more unfettered
thought, there be not less of holiness, of simplicity, of
purity, of faithful obedience to duty and to conscience,
than there was in the life of those who knew nothing of
our eager questionings, of our intellectual restlessness,
but who knew Christ, and the power of His resurrection.

" The Master stood upon the mount, and taught.
    He saw a fire in His disciples' eyes.
' The old law,' they said, ' is wholly come to nought!
    Behold the new world rise ! '

" ' Was it,' the Lord then said, ' with scorn ye saw
    The old law observed by Scribes and Pharisees ?
I say unto you, see *ye* keep that law
    More faithfully than these!

" ' Too hasty heads for ordering worlds, alas !
    Think not that I to annul the law have will'd ;
No jot, no tittle, from the law shall pass,
    Till all hath been fulfill'd.'

" So Christ said eighteen hundred years ago.
    And what, then, shall be said to those to-day
Who cry aloud to lay the old world low
    To clear the new world's way ?

" ' Religious fervours ! Ardour misapplied !
    Hence, hence,' they cry, ' ye do but keep man blind !
But keep him self-immersed, pre-occupied,
    And lame the active mind.'

" Ah ! from the old world let some one answer give :
    ' Scorn ye this world, their tears, their inward cares ?
I say unto you, see that *your* souls live
    A deeper life than theirs.' " [1]

---

[1] Matthew Arnold, " Progress."

LECTURE VIII.

THE CHURCH OF THE FUTURE.

"The spirit giveth life."—2 Cor. iii. 6.

HAVING spoken of the letter and the spirit in Scripture, in the Church, in the Sacraments, and in the Creeds, and in Christian worship and life, I propose in this last lecture to turn your thoughts mainly to the future. But before doing so, suffer me to recapitulate very briefly what I said in my fourth lecture as to the essence of the Church, and to touch for a moment on the historical position of the Church of England.

In speaking of the Christian Society, I endeavoured to show that the Church in its ideal is not a body distinguished from other religious societies by the possession of a particular form of organization, on which is dependent the due transmission of spiritual powers and influences, but simply the Christian people, united together under their Divine Head, entering into a definite relation to Him and to each other by the initiatory rite of Baptism, maintaining and renewing that relation in the Sacrament of the Lord's Supper, and possessing such a system of organization and officers as shall enable the body rightly to fulfil its functions, and shall constitute an adequate representation of the whole society.   But as in the political sphere there is the danger of the governing authority arrogating to itself an independent power, so that the king or the aristocracy or the parliament says *L'état c'est moi*, so in the ecclesiastical there is the tendency for the clergy to usurp the rights of the Church, and to say *L'église c'est nous*.   Happily, such a usurpation can confer no pre-scriptive rights.   The legal maxim which saves the rights of the crown from encroachment, *Nullum tempus occurrit regi*, might perhaps still better be read, *Nullum tempus occurrit populo*.   The idea of the Church may be overlaid and obscured by a long period of priestly domination, and the people may acquiesce in suffering their rights to be dormant; but if the Church is not dead, the Christian democracy will in time reassert itself, and the Church will once more be recognized, not as a priesthood, but as a congregation of faithful men.

Such a reassertion of the Church ideal was made in the Reformation of the sixteenth century.   We form a very inadequate idea of what the Reformation was, if we think of it simply as the shaking off of the supremacy of the Roman see, or as the mere putting away of certain abuses in discipline or of certain superstitions in worship. It was this, no doubt, and to many of the actors in the drama it may have seemed no more ; but if we look at the history of the time, not as having a thesis to main-tain, but with a desire to arrive at the truth of things,

we shall see that in its essence it was the assertion of
the lay power as against the so-called spiritualty, the
declaration of the principle that the Church is the
Christian people.

It may be objected to this view that the people were
very much passive in the movement, and that both in
England and elsewhere it was the rulers that decided
the question whether or no the Reformation should be
accepted, and, if accepted, what form it should take.[1]   It
is, of course, quite true that in the sixteenth century
what we understand by popular government did not
exist except in the Swiss cantons and in the Republic of
Geneva ; and that the personal will of the Sovereign was
the principal factor in the question.   But this does not
affect the present argument, which is that the Reformation
proceeded on the principle that each nation, represented
by its national Government, possessed the right to re-
model its Church organization, and to decide—subject
to the supreme authority of Scripture—what should be
its system of Church government and what its form of
worship.   To us of the Church of England this principle
is embodied in the Royal Supremacy.   It is difficult to
see on what ground the Sovereign can be declared to be
"over all persons, in all causes, as well ecclesiastical
as temporal, throughout his dominions supreme," or

[1] Thus the Landgrave of Hessen convoked a synod at Homberg
in 1526, to determine the future constitution of the Church in that
principality.   Cf. Hardwick, "Reformation," p. 375.   The synod
asserted for the people the right of deposing Bishops.   "Deponat
ecclesia episcopum suum, quod ad eam spectat judicare de voce
pastorum."—Schminke, "Monumenta Hassiaca," c. 23.

" supreme governor of the Church, within his dominions,"
unless it be on the ground that the Church is the nation
in its religious aspect, and that the Sovereign, as representative of the nation, is supreme over every department
of the national life. That this view was not unaccept-
able to the Bishops is shown by the fact that at the
accession of Edward VI., Cranmer and several other
Bishops took out Commissions to hold their sees during
the Royal pleasure,[1] and that in 1540 Cranmer and other
divines, in their reply to Henry VIII., distinctly speak of
civil and ecclesiastical authorities as co-ordinate under
the king :[2] "The civil ministers under the King's
Majesty in this realm of England, be those whom it
shall please his Highness for the time to put in authority
under him : as for example, the Lord Chancellor, Lord
Treasurer, Lord Great Master, Mayors, Sheriffs, etc.
The ministers of God's word, under His Majesty, be the
bishops, parsons, vicars, and such other priests as be
appointed by his Highness to that ministration : as
for example, the Bishop of Canterbury, the Bishop of
Durham, the Bishop of Winchester, the Parson of Win-
wick, etc. All the said officers and ministers, as well of
the one sort as of the other, be appointed, assigned, and
elected to every place, by the laws and orders of kings
and princes. In the admission of many of these officers
be divers comely ceremonies and solemnities used, which

---

[1] Hallam, "Const. Hist.," i., p. 100, quoting Burnet, ii. 6.
But Hardwick thinks this was only a commission empowering the
Bishops to exercise jurisdiction in their dioceses (" Reformation,"
p. 193, n. 5).

[2] Cranmer's Works, ed. Jenkyns, ii., p. 101.

be not of necessity, but only for a good order and seemly
fashion ; for if such offices and ministrations were committed without such solemnity, they were nevertheless
truly committed. And there is no more promise of God,
that grace is given in the committing of the ecclesiastical
office, than it is in the committing of the civil office."
This no doubt would appear to most persons in the
present day as pure Erastianism : nor do I quote it now
in order to commend to your acceptance the particular
view of Church authority which it appears to imply; but
only as indicating the theory on which the Reformation
of the Church of England seems to have been based by
those who were chiefly responsible for it, and the ground
which they took in separating from the Roman obedience.
Certainly from the Archiepiscopate of Cranmer to that of
Laud, we do not find that what is now called the Catholic
theory was largely present to men's minds in determining
their attitude with reference to Roman claims. No
doubt Queen Elizabeth and Archbishop Parker were
anxious to preserve all that could be preserved of the
ancient forms both of government and of worship, and
to them we owe much that is now valued by all English
Churchmen; but still it was mainly the national, and not
the wider aspect of the Church that was prominent. In
the words of Dr. Mozley : [1] " The swing of Henry VIII.'s
monarchy was simple nationalism, and nothing else ; the
nation delighted in it." And if this was true of Henry
VIII.'s, no less was it true of Elizabeth's monarchy,
especially after the Pope's excommunication and the

[1] Mozley, " Essays," i., p. 186.

Spanish Armada had roused the national spirit. The isolation of England resulting from Henry's breach with the Papal see, the masterful character of the Tudor Sovereigns, the almost theocratic character which was ascribed to the English monarchy, all these combined to impress upon the Church of England a character of nationality to which it owes many of its best and some perhaps of its worse features.[1] Even Laud's fatal attempt to revive the feudal idea of ecclesiastical power, and to call in the secular arm to enforce Church censures, was in its intention a national movement; the charge of wishing to introduce Popery was only so far true, that the King and the Archbishop were to be joint Popes : had the nation been of Laud's mind, he would have built up a compact and strong national polity in Church and State, each quite distinct, yet each supporting the other, and united together by the monarchy at the top. But the nation was not of Laud's mind, and his scheme was rudely shattered. Yet the national idea still lasted; and at the restoration of the monarchy, a very moderate concession on the part of the Bishops would have drawn the mass of the Puritans into the Church. But the reorganization of the Church was conducted on other lines, and the principle of sectarianism—the principle which asserts either that Christianity does not require and is not advanced by external unity, or that such

---

[1] "The nationality of the Church—never, we admit, fully attained—has been its most permanent and beneficent power." See an interesting essay by the Rev. G. S. Reany, Pastor of Cavendish Chapel, Manchester, in a collection of "Essays on Church Reform," published by Swan Sonnenschein and Co.

unity must consist in uniformity of belief and worship
and discipline—was accepted, and from that time forth
the idea of a national Church has dwindled into a number
of collateral religious societies, one of them claiming to
represent alone the ancient Church of England, and
the rest being the result of the free development of
individual ideas and preferences.

Few, probably, would willingly acquiesce in the
existing ecclesiastical condition of England. Few will
deny that we need to widen our conceptions of the
possibilities of Church life by looking above the actual
to the ideal. Few can look upon Christendom at large
without feeling that if Christianity is ever to develop
into a world-religion it can only be by drawing up into
itself, and appropriating whatever is good and true in
all other systems of thought and life ; by discriminating
between what is temporary and local, and what is
eternal and universal. It will not, indeed, hastily
and prematurely break with the old ; old forms are often
the best support for new life, and the healthiest life is
that in which there is least breach of continuity. As in
the individual, so in the corporate life, the child should
be father of the man. But if we believe that all
things are to be subjected unto Christ, not by a violent
catastrophe, but by the silent working of spiritual forces,
we can hardly doubt that, after all, the Church is still in
its childhood, that in many respects it still speaks as a
child, feels as a child, thinks as a child : and that the
Spirit has still to go on with the work of education,
taking of the things of Christ and declaring them to

us. Surely the marvellous expansion which science has
given to our conceptions of the physical world, the
extension of our ideas of time and space from the
chronology of Archbishop Ussher and the solar system
of Copernicus to the vast ages of time and the inter-
stellar spaces which geology and astronomy reveal to us,
may suggest that God's work in the spiritual world is
not to be measured by our standards, and that a
thousand years in His sight are but as yesterday.   And
therefore, if we may venture to speak of the future in no
spirit of confident prediction but as using that large
discourse which God has given to all of us as a means of
looking before and after, our object will be the practical
one of trying to see in what direction we ought to work,
and how we may best make the present a starting-point
for better things.

Perhaps we may anticipate that in the matter of
organization and outward form the Christian society of
the future will combine many elements that have here-
tofore been looked upon as incompatible with each other.
We cannot doubt that, on the one hand, the Catholic
theory, that the faith and the Church is everywhere one,
will find its realization ; that the belief in the Holy
Catholic Church will no longer be understood as a
declaration that he who professes it is claiming fellowship with a definitely limited body of Christians, and
marking himself off from others ; that the body of
Christ will more and more tend to become co-extensive
with that redeemed humanity of which Christ is the
head.   And yet, just as the consciousness of the unity

of the race does not abolish national and tribal and
family distinctions, but only subordinates them to a
higher conception, even so the consciousness that the
Catholic Church is wider than all our limitations will
not obscure the boundaries of national and local
Churches, but will set them in their proper dependence
under the wider and higher idea. And if once we have
received into our minds that wider idea, we shall find
it less difficult to be patient and tolerant of all those
narrow and inadequate conceptions which have taken its
place. "The dissidence of Dissent"—that is, indeed,
not an inspiring ideal: one would rather say, " I believe
in the Holy Catholic Church," even if in so saying one
only meant, " I believe in Episcopally governed Christendom," than, " I believe in the dissidence of Dissent."
But at the same time we cannot close our eyes to the
fact, that the spirit of individualism which has led the
Christian people of Great Britain to segregate themselves
into 180 religious denominations,[1] has its place in the
economy of God's providence, and that at any rate a
living sectarianism is better than a dead uniformity.
And in the same way, we cannot but believe that of the
great religious denominations, from the Roman Church
to the Society of Friends, every one has some contribu-
tion to bring to the building up of the Church that is to
be; that they are destined, not to be destroyed or cast as
rubbish to the void, but to be drawn up and gradually
assimilated into the wider and more healthy and more
fruitful social life. And the great practical thought that

[1] " Statesman's Year-book for 1888."

forces itself upon us in this connexion is, that we should none of us be content to acquiesce in the present condition of religious disintegration. The Master's desire " that they all may be one," can never be held to be satisfied by His disciples sitting down in little groups of believers and regarding each other with benevolent sentiments. For think only for one instant of the waste of power which such a theory involves. Think of the rival missionary societies, home and foreign ; think of the overlapping organizations, religious, philanthropic, educational ; think of a small area having one set of Church institutions, two or three sets of Nonconformist institutions, and another set of undenominational institutions. Would it be possible for us to accept such a state of things as tolerable, if we had not sophisticated our minds into the belief that it is the best attainable ?

I know that there will be those, perhaps even in this congregation, who will be ready to say, " There is a perfectly simple and easy solution to the difficulty. Disestablish and disendow the Church of England, and all denominations will fall into each other's arms, indifferentism will disappear, and the kingdom of Heaven will be realized." It is clearly impossible to devote even a fragment of my last lecture to an argument on this subject ; I can only state my own firm conviction that the result of this policy would be the accentuating and embittering of religious rivalries to an extent that would dispose men who care for a religion of soberness and peace to stand aloof from religious organizations, and to leave them to be fought over by fanatics. Even in countries where no established Church has existed the same ecclesiastical rivalries are found ; but if to other causes of rivalry were added a great and powerful Church, with a smarting sense of wrong, eager to regain in influence what it had lost in position, no longer restrained from aggressive proselytism by a sense of responsibility to the nation, it seems probable that sectarian animosities, far from being mitigated, would be increased tenfold.

But to return. We cannot under any reasonable theory acquiesce in a Christendom of sectarianism. We must pray for a united Christendom. And if, besides praying for it, we are to work towards it, it will not be superfluous to ask, What is likely to be the basis of the Christian society of the future ?

Experience does not encourage us to expect that the bases of religious association which have hitherto prevailed will serve as the foundations of the future temple. Identity of religious belief may be a strong, but it is not a wide-reaching bond of religious union. Indeed, the more keen is the interest in theology, the more inadequate will it be found as the basis of union : men's minds are differently constituted ; they see things in different proportions ; they approach them from opposite sides. The only way in which doctrine could be made the primary ground of union would be by men accepting without inquiry the authority of an infallible Church ; and to those who study the signs of the times this will hardly appear a probable solution of the difficulty.

Nor are men likely to unite on the basis of Church organization. The history of the Church before the Reformation is surely a sufficient indication that mere uniformity of external government is no guarantee for spiritual life; in the words of Baxter,[1] " This unity in meer Profession is properly no Christian unity. . . . If this be all, it is but in the bark and shell that we are agreed; it is but a seeming agreement, from the teeth outwards." It is a mistake indeed to disparage and undervalue organic unity; the disorganized state of Christendom paralyzes Christian work, and makes us weak in the presence of the enemy : but such unity must be the product and result of the unity of the Spirit working from within outwards, producing in men's minds that sense of Christian brotherhood which will gradually draw them together into a closer union. For any body of Christians to say, " We, and we only, possess the true and legitimate form of Church order, therefore it is the duty of all who would be members of the one body to conform to our model," is more likely to perpetuate disunion than to draw Christians together.

What, then, is the most promising basis on which Christians can unite ? If we go back to the origins of Christianity, we shall find that the Church was preeminently a beneficent organization. The fervour of the first disciples at Jerusalem led them to unite in a sort of religious communism : " All that believed were together, and had all things common; and they sold their possessions and goods, and parted them to all,

---

[1] Baxter's " Catholic Unity," p. 203.

according as any man had need." The earliest Church office, that of the diaconate, was clearly for purposes of beneficence.[1] To minister to the saints was an acknowledged and universal duty. St. Paul's journeys were to some extent governed by his plans for the mutual assistance of the Churches. He makes the dependence of Christians on each other a fundamental principle of the Church. And this being so, is it not at least possible that, as Christian association found its first basis in beneficence, so the remedy for our unhappy divisions may be found rather in the principle of association for philanthropic purposes than in a common theology or a common ritual or a common organization? "See how these Christians love one another," was a tribute of admiration extorted from observers without by the mutual helpfulness of the primitive Church; may not a similar devotion to good works on a yet larger and more comprehensive scale be a means towards restoring that unity which perished in the attempt to enforce uniformity of belief and observance? Certainly the present age would seem to favour such a hope. For there is springing up now a certain enthusiasm of humanity, an impatience of preventable suffering, an eagerness to make the life of the less-favoured classes brighter, healthier, more natural, which points to the possibility of a new social crusade against ignorance, against vice, against the evils that oppress and darken the lives of the helpless classes. It is a thing to be thankful for,

---

[1] See Bishop Lightfoot's "Essay on the Christian Ministry," and Dr. Hatch's "Bampton Lectures."

that in an age of religious unsettlement, when so many of the more thoughtful men have drifted from the old moorings, there should be this rallying point in a new and healthy interest in social reforms : if the Church of Christ is in its ideal a world-wide society in which the strong are to bear the burdens of the weak, and the rich are to hold their wealth in trust for the poor, then such an enthusiasm of philanthropy as that which our age is witnessing is surely a hopeful augury for Christianity. It may be that for the time men do not recognize it as Christian ; they may call it altruism, the service of humanity, or what they will ; but as Christ said to His disciples, " He that is not against us is on our part," so now surely He would claim as His disciples all whose aim is not to be ministered unto but to minister ; He would say, " Forbid them not ; for there is no man which shall do a mighty work in My Name, and be able quickly to speak evil of Me." It is surely a hopeful sign in Oxford, that, whereas fifty years ago the energy and intellectual activity of the University was wholly absorbed by theological controversy, now much of it is directed into the more fruitful and more Christian channel of social improvement. University settlements in East London, college missions in the midst of artisan populations, educational movements to reach the middle class,—these, and other like signs of the times, show that Oxford is not unmindful of the Christian maxim, " To whom much is given, of them shall much be required." It is true that the formal and official aspect of religion is less prominent here than it was a generation ago ; it

is true that subscription to the Thirty-nine Articles is
no longer a condition of membership in the University ;
it is true that the foundations are open to men of
any and of no religious belief : but if men are learning
here the lesson of effort for the good of others, the
lesson of responsibility for their brother-men, if they
are learning that we are members one of another, and
that if one member suffer all the members suffer with
it, then let us not dare to say that Oxford is no longer
a place of Christian education ; for what education can
be more Christian than that which teaches men to follow
the example of our Saviour Christ, and to be made like
unto Him ?

And if this is the case in Oxford, it is not less so
among serious-minded men elsewhere. The old Latin
rime says that Oxford controversies soon spread over the
country :—

> " Chronica si penses, cum pugnant Oxonienses,
> Post paucos menses volat ira per Angligenenses."

Surely we may hope that when the University turns its
mind to more peaceful interests, its example will spread
in this respect too, and that an intelligent and unselfish
interest in social problems will be more and more characteristic of the age in which we live. There is work
enough and to spare for all. Let us not doubt that in
working for our brethren we are working for Christ;
for He Himself has said, " Inasmuch as ye did it unto
one of these My brethren, even these least, ye did it
unto Me."

Such a basis of Church unity is more adapted to the

conditions of the present day than a dogmatic or an
institutional one. For ours is a democratic age, and no
system, either religious or political, can hope to stand
which does not rest upon a broad foundation of popular
interest. And it seems certain that men in the present
day are more likely to be interested in social and moral
problems than in the more abstract questions of theology.
Assuredly, if the Christian Church is to be a real power
in the world, it can only be by frankly and unreservedly
throwing herself upon the people. It is no longer possible for the Church to rely upon traditional reverence or
upon high-sounding claims ; but if she will set herself,
in her Master's spirit, "to preach good tidings to the
poor, to proclaim release to the captives, and recover-
ing of sight to the blind, to set at liberty them that are
bruised, to proclaim the acceptable year of the Lord,"
there is no limit to the possibilities that are before
her. If she will not timidly confine herself to a narrow
circle of so-called religious duties, but will boldly claim
as her own all human interests—*humani nihil a se
alienum putans*—she may yet set forth the religion of
the Son of Man as the religion of humanity, and may
show that the service of Christ is indeed the service of
man.

I endeavoured in a former lecture to show that
Christian theology, being man's conception of God and
of his own relation to God, is a progressive science,
and that God's revelation of Himself was not closed
with the completion of the Canon of the New Testament.
If we believe that all light and knowledge have their

source in God, we cannot doubt that to this our age
God has revealed and is revealing Himself very specially.
And it is vain to say that science does not come into
contact with religion. There is absolutely no section of
the Church and no school of thought that has not been
consciously, or perhaps more often unconsciously, affected
by modern knowledge and modern methods. It is not
so much that any particular discovery has upset this or
that theory of Scripture interpretation or system of evidences, but rather that there has been a general though
gradual onward movement, and it is only by looking
back that we can see how great the advance has been.
Who would now maintain the letter of the Mosaic
cosmogony against the conclusions of geology and
astronomy? Who would now apply to the Bible,
words spoken from this pulpit within the recollection
of many of us : " Every book of it, every chapter of it,
every verse of it, every word of it, every syllable of it,
—(*where* are we to *stop?*)—every letter of it is the
direct utterance of the Most High ? " [1] Who would
now refuse to recognize discrepancies and inaccuracies
even in the Gospel narratives ? Who would now make
miracles the primary evidence of Christianity, as was
generally done by the writers of the last century ? And
yet, is Christianity less operative, less influential, less
of a motive force than it formerly was ? Do men care
less for the spirit of the Bible, because the superstitious
reverence for its letter has been overthrown ? And if
this process has gone on in the past, may we not reason-

[1] Burgon, " Inspiration and Interpretation," p. 89.

ably conclude that it will go on in the future? It is not
for us, indeed, to forecast the working of the Spirit of
God in the minds of men ; but yet we can hardly doubt
that it will be in the direction of a more spiritual conception of God and of His kingdom, and that, as in the
past so in the future, men will find that the things
which they have contended over, and for which they
have persecuted each other, are really but the outside
expression of religion, and that the things which seemed
to them too simple to be dwelt upon, are, after all, the
things that are eternal. For experience teaches us that
it is the simple things that are the great things ; and as
we grow older we learn a new sense of proportion and
a new measure of the importance of doctrine. As Baxter
says, " I value all things according to their use and end.
That is the best Doctrine and Study which maketh men
better, and tendeth to make them happy." [1]

Surely the lesson that we need is to have faith in
God ; to trust not in our own formulas and systems, not
in spasmodic revivals, but in the power of the living
God. We are too apt to identify the kingdom of God
with our preconceived theories ; and then, if our theories
fail, we think that the gates of hell have prevailed, and
that God's cause is lost. But God's cause does not
depend upon our theories, and it will outlive them.
And it is a law of God's kingdom, that all spiritual
progress demands sacrifice. [2] The Jew before entering
Christ's kingdom had to give up the letter of the Old

[1] Baxter's " Life and Times," p. 127.
[2] Cf. Westcott's " Christus Consummator," pp. 4, 5.

Covenant and the worship of his forefathers, and to surrender his exclusive position, and to welcome as brethren those whom he had regarded as beyond the reach of God's favour. But he gained the power of knowing and worshipping the spiritual Christ. Luther had to go through a fierce struggle in breaking with the monastic life and the traditions of his education to fight the battle of Christian freedom. But the sacrifice of the letter enabled him to rise to the religion of the spirit, and to assert the priesthood of the Christian people. And so it may be that we shall have to sacrifice some of our prepossessions, some of the things which we have identified with Christ's religion, some of the oldness of the letter, in order to accept the newness of the spirit. Only let us be patient; let us not be over-anxious to have a complete theory, that stands four-square on all points; let us be content to wait for more light; let us ask that we may have ears to hear and eyes to see and hearts to understand God's progressive revelation in science, in the widening interpretation of Scripture, in the growth of new social and industrial types. And let us beware of caring more for our own views or our own special organization, than for the promotion of right and well-being and good living. Let us beware of the temptation to postpone truth and justice to religion and piety.

The history of religious thought may well teach us modesty and forbearance. How often has it happened that the views which one generation proscribes as dangerous the next tolerates, and the third accepts as

truth ! How often have divines rushed to protest
against opinions which their successors have defended as
harmless ! Evolution, which not many years ago was
solemnly denounced in Oxford by an eloquent Bishop
and a popular statesman, is now maintained as consistent with the most unblemished orthodoxy. Yes, not
only the blood of the martyrs but sometimes even the
ashes of the heretics may claim to be the seed of the
Church.

And if our modes of thought, no less do our external
methods require adaptation to the needs of a new age.
We can hardly doubt, for instance, that if the older
Churches are to hold their own in the new world, it
must be by learning from their younger sisters the secret
of popularizing their institutions. The Church of
England in particular, from no fault of her own but by
the force of circumstances, has drifted into a position
which is hardly tolerable, in which the minister of each
parish is practically autocratic, while the people are
purely passive and receptive. This is not the occasion
for suggesting remedies for this evil ; but assuredly, if
the Church of England is to continue to be the only
organized society in the country whose members have no
opportunity of giving effect to their deliberate judgment,
it can hardly be but that much of the religious energy
and thoughtfulness of the age will cease to flow in the
ancient bed of the stream, and will find other and freer
channels for itself.

And as at home, so too in its relations to those that
are without, the Church must learn more modern

methods. When the Church first became conscious of responsibility in relation to the heathen, the idea of missions was a simple one. It was, first to proclaim to them that they were perishing, and that their only hope lay in the acceptance of the Christian faith ; and then to offer them our organization, our forms of worship, our doctrinal formulas, our highly developed type of European Christianity.[1] It is not surprising that the attempt to convert Orientals into English Churchmen or Scottish Presbyterians or American Baptists should have met with but moderate success. It would surely be more in accordance with the Apostolic model to set before men the Christianity of the New Testament in its simplest form—Christ as the revelation of the Father, the Spirit as the indwelling of God in man, with perhaps some rudimentary and provisional organization, and then to leave the vital principle to develop an outward framework such as might be adapted to its environment. The more suitable our English type of Christianity may be to Englishmen, the less is it likely to meet the requirements of men of other races.

I have endeavoured, in these lectures, to bring out according to my power the distinction between the permanent and the transitory, between the essential and the accidental, in the Christian religion and life. It is a great subject, and no one can be more conscious than I am how much has been left unsaid, how much might

---

[1] Cf. a sermon on the "Evangelization of India," preached before the University in 1857, by Rev. G. H. Curteis, Fellow of Exeter College.

have been better said. It is a question beset with
difficulties, but it is one on the solution of which
depends the future of Christianity. It is one on which
there will be many different judgments, and which
demands candour, mutual forbearance, and an honest
endeavour to look at it from all points of view. The
temper required is, as was said in a former lecture, that
of the householder who bringeth forth out of his treasure
things new and old. We must not, indeed, cling to the
old because it is old, nor yet grasp at the new because it
is new ; we must try to preserve and keep fresh what is
good in the old, and to welcome and use to the utmost
what is true in the new. And have not we of the
Church of England a very special advantage in this
respect ? Combining as we do the stateliness of the
ancient formularies with much of freedom of thought,
much of flexibility and capacity for adaptation ; the letter
of the ancient confessions with the spirit of modern
inquiry ; uniting, as we do, in one communion men of the
most opposite temper—men reverencing the old, like Dr.
Pusey, and men eagerly welcoming the new, like Arthur
Stanley,—are not we marked out by our very position
and inheritance to mediate between the past and the
future, to turn the hearts of the fathers to the children,
and the hearts of the children to their fathers ; to
temper the eager impetuosity of youth with the calm
wisdom of old age ? Yes, upon us is laid by God's
providence the great work of claiming for Christ the
science, the criticism, the philosophy, the democratic life
of the new age ; of so welding together the old and the

new, that there may be no breach of continuity, no
revolutionary shock, but that the new social and
intellectual life of England may be not less but more
Christian than that of our forefathers. "We have heard
with our ears, O God, our fathers have told us, what
Thou hast done in their time of old;" and if we have
faith, and doubt not, He has yet greater things in store
for us, and for our children.

I concluded my first lecture with a word of advice
to you, my younger hearers. Suffer me to address you
once more in concluding my last. I warned you then
against trusting to the letter, against the tendency to
make religion too much a matter of system and organization. Let me warn you to-day against too hastily
dispensing with outward helps. What strikes one most
in modern Oxford is the almost total relaxation of
academical discipline. It may be that there was too
much of it in days gone by ; it may be that there is too
little of it now. But however this may be, it lays on
you the responsibility of disciplining your own life. If
your life is to flow in a strong concentrated current, and
to overbear obstacles, you must build strong barriers to
prevent its spreading all abroad and losing itself in
shallows. " Self-reverence, self-knowledge, self-control "
—that is what you must aim at. And the best helps to
these things are the old and simple ones—prayer, the
intelligent study of Scripture, self-recollectedness, communion with Christ. Let me conclude with the glowing
words addressed to the young men of his day by one
who was dear to many of us, words which some here
may remember.

" Be as free, be as liberal, be as courageous as you
will ; but be religious, *because* you are liberal ; be
devout, *because* you are free ; be pure, *because* you are
bold ; cast away the works of darkness, *because* you are
the children of light ; be humble, and considerate, and
forbearing, *because* you are charged with hopes as grand
as were ever committed to the rising generation of any
Church or of any country. These hopes are for you to
destroy or to fulfil. On you, more than on any other force
or power amongst us, depends the life and soul of any
true, Christian, manly progress in Oxford or in
England." [1]

And now I bring this course of sermons to a close. If
anything has been said contrary to God's Will, may He
pardon and blot it out ; if anything in accordance with
His Will, may He accept and make it fruitful. " Domine
Deus, quæcunque dixi de tuo, agnoscant et tui ; si qua
de meo, et Tu ignosce et tui."

ADDITIONAL NOTE TO LECTURE VIII.

I venture to append to this Lecture the eloquent passage in
which Dean Milman, in the peroration of his " Latin Christianity,"
speaks of the future of Teutonic Christianity :—

" Its intellectual faith will be more robust; nor will its emo-
tional be less profound and intense. But the strength of its
intellectual faith (and herein is at once its glory and its danger)
will know no limits to its daring speculation. How far Teutonic
Christianity may in some parts already have gone almost or absolutely beyond the pale of Christianity, how far it may have lost

---

[1] " Great Opportunities." A farewell sermon preached before
the University of Oxford on Advent Sunday, 1863, by Arthur
Penrhyn Stanley, D.D.

itself in its unrebuked wanderings, posterity only will know. What distinctness of conception, what precision of language may be indispensable to true faith ; what part of the ancient dogmatic system may be allowed silently to fall into disuse, as at least superfluous, and as beyond the proper range of human thought and human language ; how far the sacred records may, without real peril to their truth, be subjected to closer investigation ; to what wider interpretation, especially of the Semitic portion, those records may submit, and wisely submit, in order to harmonize them with the irrefutable conclusions of science ; how far the Eastern veil of allegory which hangs over their truth may be lifted or torn away to show their unshadowed essence ; how far the poetic vehicle through which truth is conveyed may be gently severed from the truth ;—all this must be left to the future historian of our religion. As it is my own confident belief that the words of Christ, and His words alone (the primal, indefeasible truths of Christianity), shall not pass away ; so I cannot presume to say that men may not attain to a clearer, at the same time more full and comprehensive and balanced sense of those words, than has as yet been generally received in the Christian world. As all else is transient and mutable, these only eternal and universal, assuredly, whatever light may be thrown on the mental constitution of man, even on the constitution of nature, and the laws which govern the world, will be concentered so as to give a more penetrating vision of those undying truths. Teutonic Christianity (and this seems to be its mission and privilege), however nearly in its more perfect form it may already have approximated, may approximate still more closely to the absolute and perfect faith of Christ ; it may discover and establish the sublime unison of religion and reason ; keep in tone the triple-chorded harmony of faith, holiness, and charity ; assert its own freedom, know the bounds of that freedom, respect the freedom of others. Christianity may yet have to exercise a far wider, even if more silent and untraceable influence, through its primary, all-penetrating, all-pervading principles, on the civilization of mankind."

To this I would add a passage from a less-known writing of the same author, the sermon on "Hebrew Prophecy," preached before the University in 1865 :—

"Of the future of Christianity what Christian will presume to despair ? May not that future be the more complete redintegration of that eternal union, the more solemn ratification, as it were,

of that heaven-blessed marriage sacrament, the more perfect fusion
of the religious and moral elements of our faith? We may believe
not less profoundly, though we believe in a more Christian spirit.
As it will most need, so the highest civilization will submit, and
only submit, to a Christianity which has shaken off all unworthy
superstitions, the encrustation of ages upon its simpler doctrines.
. . . I cannot and will not believe but that the advancement of
mankind in arts, in science, in knowledge, in the knowledge of
itself, the history of our race, the limits of our intellectual faculties,
the powers of our language, in the intercommunion of family with
family of nations, in civil and religious liberty, and in all that
expands and elevates our being, will eventually harmonize and enter
into closer fellowship with the religion of Christ."

APPENDIX

It has been thought that the following brief account of the founder of the Bampton Lectures, and of the Lectures themselves, may be interesting.

John Bampton was born in 1689. He was educated at Trinity College, Oxford, where he graduated B.A. in 1709, and M.A. in 1712. Having taken Orders, he was in 1718 collated to the prebend of *Minor pars altaris* in the cathedral church of Salisbury, which preferment he held till his death in 1751. He left his lands and estates to found the Bampton Lectures; an extract from his will is prefixed to each year's volume of lectures. His bequest did not take effect till 1779, twenty-eight years after his death, when the first lecturer was chosen. At this time the estates produced a yearly income of £120.

The following are the names of the preachers and their subjects. Although the founder provides that the lecturer shall be of the degree of Master of Arts, at least, in one of the Universities of Oxford or Cambridge, it does not appear that any Cambridge man was appointed until the year 1874—

1780. James Bandinel, D.D., Jesus. "The Peculiar Doctrines of Christianity."

1781. Timothy Neve, D.D., Merton. "Jesus Christ the Saviour of the World and Redeemer of Mankind."

1782. Robert Holmes, M.A., New College. "On the Prophecies and Testimony of John the Baptist and the Parallel Prophecies of Jesus Christ."

1783. John Cobb, D.D., St. John's. "An Enquiry after Happiness : Natural Religion, the Gospel, etc."

1784. Jos. White, B.D., Wadham. "A Comparison of Christianity and Mohammedanism in their History, their Evidence, and their Effects."

1785. Ralph Churton, M.A., Brasenose. "On the Prophecies respecting the Destruction of Jerusalem."

1786. George Croft, D.D., University. "The Use and Abuse of Reason; Objections against Inspiration considered; the Authority of the Ancient Fathers examined, etc."

1787. William Hawkins, M.A., Pembroke. "On Scripture Mysteries."

1788. Richard Shepherd, D.D., Corpus. "The Ground and Credibility of the Christian Religion."

1789. Edward Tatham, D.D., Lincoln. "The Chart and Scale of Truth." 2 vols.

1790. Henry Kett, M.A., Trinity. "The Conduct and Opinions of the Primitive Christians, with Remarks on Gibbon and Priestley."

1791. Robert Morres, M.A., Brasenose. "On Faith in General, etc."

1792. John Eveleigh, D.D., Provost of Oriel. "The Substance, History, and Evidences of our Religion."

1793. James Williamson, B.D., Queen's. "The Truth, Inspiration, Authority, and Evidence of the Scriptures considered and defended."

1794. Thomas Wintle, B.D., Pembroke. "The Expediency, Prediction, and Accomplishment of the Christian Redemption illustrated."

1795. Daniel Veysie, B.D., Oriel. "The Doctrine of Atonement illustrated and defended."

1796. Robert Gray, M.A., St. Mary Hall. "The Principles upon which the Reformation of the Church of England was established."

1797. W. Finch, D.C.L., St. John's. "The Objection of Infidel Historians and other Writers against Christianity considered."

1798. Charles Henry Hall, B.D., Christ Church. "Fulness of Time; or the Steps by which Almighty God gradually prepared the Way for the Introduction and Promulgation of the Gospel."

1799. William Barrow, D.C.L., Queen's. "Answers to some Popular Objections against the Necessity or Credibility of the Christian Revelation."

1800. G. Richards, M.A., Oriel. "The Divine Origin of Prophecy illustrated and defended."

1801. George Stanley Faber, M.A., Lincoln. "Horæ Mosaicæ; or a View of the Mosaical Records, with Respect to their Coincidence with Profane Antiquity, their Internal Credibility, and their Connexion with Christianity." 2 vols.

1802. George Frederick Nott, B.D., All Souls. "Religious Enthusiasm." (This course was directed against Wesley and Whitfield.)

1803. John Farrer, M.A., Queen's. "On the Mission and Character of Christ, and on the Beatitudes."

1804. Richard Lawrence, D.C.L., University. "An Attempt to Illustrate those Articles of the Church of England which the Calvinists improperly consider as Calvinistical."

1805. Edward Nares, M.A., Merton. "A View of the Evidences of Christianity at the Close of the Pretended Age of Reason."

1806. J. Brown, M.A., Corpus. "The Infancy of Human Nature."

1807. Thomas Le Mesurier, M.A., New College. "The Nature and Guilt of Schism considered with a Particular Reference to the Principles of the Reformation."

1808. J. Penrose, M.A., Corpus. "An Attempt to prove the Truth of Christianity from the Wisdom displayed in its Original Establishment, and from the History of False and Corrupted Systems of Religion."

1809. J. B. S. Carwithen, M.A., St. Mary Hall. "A View of the Brahminical Religion in its Confirmation of the Truth of the Sacred History, and in its Influence on the Moral Character."

1810. T. Falconer, M.A., Corpus. "Certain Principles in 'Evanson's 'Dissonance of the Four generally received Evangelists, etc.' examined."

1811. J. Bidlake, D.D., Christ Church. "The Truth and Consistency of Divine Revelation, with some Remarks on the Contrary Extremes of Infidelity and Enthusiasm."

1812. Richard Mant, M.A., Oriel. "An Appeal to the Gospel; or, an Inquiry into the Justice of the Charge, alleged by the Methodists and other Objectors, that the Gospel is not preached by the National Clergy."

1813. J. Collinson, M.A., Queen's. "A Key to the Writings of the Principal Fathers of the Christian Church who flourished during the First Three Centuries."

P

1814. William Van Mildert, D.D., Christ Church. An Inquiry into the General Principles of Scripture Interpretation."

1815. Reginald Heber, M.A., All Souls. "The Personality and Office of the Christian Comforter asserted and explained."

1816. John Hume Spry, M.A., Oriel. "Christian Unity doctrinally and historically considered."

1817. John Miller, M.A., Worcester. "The Divine Authority of Holy Scripture asserted, from its Adaptation to the Real State of Human Nature."

1818. Charles Abel Moysey, M.A., Christ Church. "The Doctrines of the Unitarians examined as opposed to the Church of England."

1819. Hector Davies Morgan, M.A., Trinity. "A Compressed View of the Religious Principles and Practices of the Age; or, a Trial of the Chief Spirits that are in the World by the Standard of the Scriptures."

1820. Godfrey Faussett, M.A., Magdalen. "The Claims of the Established Church to Exclusive Attachment and Support, and the Dangers which menace her from Schism and Indifference."

1821. John Jones, M.A., Jesus. "The Moral Tendency of Divine Revelation asserted and illustrated."

1822. Richard Whately, M.A., Oriel. "The Use and Abuse of Party-feeling in Matters of Religion."

1823. C. Goddard, D.D., Christ Church. "The Mental Condition necessary to a Due Inquiry into Religious Evidence, stated and exemplified."

1824. John Josias Conybeare, M.A., Christ Church. "An Attempt to trace the History and ascertain the Limits of the Secondary and Spiritual Interpretation of Scripture."

1825. George Chandler, D.C.L., New College. "The Scheme of Divine Revelation considered principally in its Connexion with the Progress and Improvement of Human Society."

1826. William Vaux, M.A., Balliol. "The Benefits annexed to a Participation in the Two Christian Sacraments of Baptism and the Lord's Supper."

1827. Henry Hart Milman, M.A., Brasenose. "The Character and Conduct of the Apostles, considered as an Evidence of Christianity."

1828. Thomas Horne, B.D., Christ Church. "The Religious Necessity of the Reformation asserted, and the Extent to which it was carried in the Church of England vindicated."

1829. Edward Burton, D.D., Christ Church. "The Heresies of the Apostolic Age."

1830. Henry Soames, M.A., Wadham. "The Doctrines of the Anglo Saxon Church."

1831. T. W. Lancaster, M.A., Queen's. "The Popular Evidence of Christianity stated and explained."

1832. Renn Dickson Hampden, M.A., Oriel. "The Scholastic Philosophy considered in its Relation to Christian Theology."

1833. Fred. Nolan, D.C.L., Exeter. "The Analogy of Revelation and Science established."

1834. No appointment.

1835. No appointment.

1836. Charles Atmore Ogilvie, M.A., Balliol. "The Divine Glory manifested in the Conduct and Discourses of our Lord."

1837. Thomas Stuart Lyle Vogan, M.A., St. Edmund's Hall. "The Principal Objections against the Doctrine of the Trinity, and a Portion of the Evidence on which that Doctrine is received by the Catholic Church reviewed."

1838. Henry A. Woodgate, B.D., St. John's. "The Authoritative Teaching of the Church shown to be in Conformity with Scripture, Analogy, and the Moral Constitution of Man."

1839. William D. Conybeare, M.A., Christ Church. "An Analytical Examination of the Character, etc., of the Christian Fathers during the Ante-Nicene Period."

1840. Edward Hawkins, D.D., Provost of Oriel. "An Enquiry into the Connected Uses of the Principal Means of attaining Christian Truth."

1841. Samuel Wilberforce, M.A., Oriel. (No lectures delivered, owing to a domestic affliction.)

1842. James Garbett, M.A., Brasenose. "Christ, as Prophet, Priest, and King; being a Vindication of the Church of England from Theological Novelties."

1843. Anthony Grant, D.C.L., New College. "The Past and Prospective Extension of the Gospel by Missions to the Heathen."

1844. Richard William Jelf, D.D., Canon of Christ Church. "An Inquiry into the Means of Grace, their Mutual Connexion and Combined Use, with Especial Reference to the Church of England."

1845. Charles Abel Heurtley, B.D., Corpus. "Justification."

1846. Augustus Short, M.A., Christ Church. "The Witness of the Spirit with our Spirit."

1847. Right Rev. Walter Augustus Shirley, D.D., New College. "The Supremacy of Holy Scripture." (This course was not completed, owing to the death of the lecturer.)

1848. Edward Garrard Marsh, M.A., Oriel. "The Christian Doctrine of Sanctification considered."

1849. Richard Michell, B.D., Lincoln. "The Nature and Comparative Value of the Christian Evidences considered generally."

1850. Edward Meyrick Goulburn, M.A., Merton. "The Doctrine of the Resurrection of the Same Body as taught in Holy Scripture."

1851. Henry Bristow Wilson, B.D., St. John's. "The Communion of Saints. An Attempt to illustrate the True Principles of Christian Union."

1852. Joseph Esmond Riddle, M.A., St. Edmund Hall. "The Natural History of Infidelity and Superstition in contrast with Christian Faith."

1853. William Thomson, M.A., Queen's. "The Atoning Work of Christ, viewed in Relation to some Current Theories."

1854. Hon. Samuel Waldegrave, M.A., All Souls. "New Testament Millenarianism; or, the Kingdom and Coming of Christ, as taught by Himself and His Apostles."

1855. J. E. Bode, M.A. Christ Church. "The Absence of Precision in the Formularies of the Church of England Scriptural, and suitable to a State of Probation."

1856. Edward A. Litton, M.A., Oriel. "The Mosaic Dispensation considered as Introductory to Christianity."

1857. William Edward Jelf, B.D., Christ Church. "Christian Faith, Comprehensive, not Partial; Definite, not Uncertain."

1858. H. Longueville Mansel, B.D., St. John's. "The Limits of Religious Thought examined."

1859. George Rawlinson, M.A., Exeter. "The Historical Evidences of the Truth of the Scripture Records, stated anew, with Special Reference to the Doubts and Discoveries of Modern Times."

1860. James Augustus Hessey, D.C.L., St. John's. "Sunday: its Origin, History, and Present Obligation."

1861. John Sandford, B.D., Balliol. "The Mission and Extension of the Church at Home."

1862. Adam Storey Farrar, M.A., Queen's. "A Critical History of Free Thought in Reference to the Christian Religion."

1863. John Hannah, D.C.L., Lincoln. "The Relation between the Divine and Human Elements in Holy Scripture."

1864. Thomas Dehany Bernard, M.A., Exeter. "The Progress of Doctrine in the New Testament."

1865. James B. Mozley, B.D., Magdalen. "Miracles."

1866. Henry Parry Liddon, D.D., Christ Church. "The Divinity of our Lord and Saviour Jesus Christ."

1867. E. Garbett, M.A., Pembroke. "Dogmatic Faith."

1868. G. Moberly, D.C.L., Balliol. "The Administration of the Holy Spirit in the Body of Christ."

1869. R. Payne Smith., D.D., Canon of Christ Church. "Prophecy a Preparation for Christ."

1870. William J. Irons, D.D., Queen's. "Christianity as taught by St. Paul."

1871. George H. Curteis, M.A., Exeter. "Dissent in its Relation to the Church of England."

1872. J. R. T. Eaton, M.A., Merton. "The Permanence of Christianity."

1873. Isaac Gregory Smith, M.A., Brasenose. "Characteristics of Christian Morality."

1874. Stanley Leathes, M.A., Jesus College, Cambridge. "The Religion of Christ, its Historic and Literary Development Evidence of its Origin."

1875. W. Jackson, M.A., Worcester. "The Doctrine of Retribution."

1876. Right Rev. William Alexander, D.D., Brasenose. "The Witness of the Psalms to Christ."

1877. C. A. Row, M.A., Pembroke. "Christian Evidence and Modern Thought."

1878. C. H. H. Wright, M.A., Exeter. "Zechariah and his Prophecies, considered in Relation to Modern Criticism."

1879. H. Wace, M.A., Brasenose. "The Foundations of Faith."

1880. Edwin Hatch, M.A., Pembroke. "The Organization of the Early Christian Churches."

1881. John Wordsworth, M.A., Brasenose. "The One Religion."

1882. Peter Goldsmith Medd, M.A., University. "The One Mediator. The Operation of the Son of God in Nature and in Grace."

1883. Hon. William Henry Fremantle, M.A., Balliol. "The World as the Subject of Redemption."

1884. Right Rev. Frederick Temple, D.D., Balliol. "The Relations between Religion and Science."

1885. Frederick William Farrar, D D., Trinity College, Cambridge. "The History of Interpretation."

1886. Charles Bigg, D.D., Corpus. "The Christian Platonists of Alexandria."

1887. Right Rev. William Boyd Carpenter, D.D., St. Katherine's College, Cambridge. "The Permanent Elements of Religion."

1888. Robert Edward Bartlett, M.A., Trinity. "The Letter and the Spirit."